THE USUAL SUSPECTS

Christopher McQuarrie

ff

faber and faber

First published in 1996
by Faber and Faber Limited
3 Queen Square London WC1N 3AU

This edition published in 2000

Photoset by Parker Typesetting Service, Leicester
Printed and bound in Great Britain by
Mackays of Chatham PLC, Chatham, Kent

A CIP record for this book
is available from the British Library

ISBN 0-571-20325-6

2 4 6 8 10 9 7 5 3 1

CONTENTS

INTRODUCTION

Christopher McQuarrie interviewed by Todd Lippy

Christopher McQuarrie was born in 1968 in Princeton Junction, New Jersey, where he attended high school with director Bryan Singer. He spent his first year out of school working abroad at a boarding school in West Australia before returning to the US to work at a detective agency in New Jersey for the next four years.

In 1991, he was approached by Singer to co-write the screenplay for their first feature film, *Public Access*, which went on to win the Grand Jury Prize at the 1993 Sundance Film Festival. In the ensuing year, McQuarrie wrote *The Usual Suspects*, which premièred at the 1995 Sundance Festival, and was also featured in the '*Un certain regard*' section of the 1995 Cannes Film Festival. McQuarrie lives in Los Angeles, and is currently at work on several projects, including another film with Singer.

The version of *The Usual Suspects* published here is McQuarrie's final draft, completed in the Fall of 1993.

How did you get into screenwriting in the first place?
Bryan Singer [director of *The Usual Suspects*, and director and co-screenwriter of *Public Access*] and I knew each other from the time we were very little; our parents were friends. I had been in one of his 8mm films – I'd always kind of known him, but we'd never really been close. It was after he graduated from high school – he was two years ahead of me – that we really became friends. He was talking with another friend about making an anthology film and there was a script that they were putting together. One of the stories was based on something I had written. Bryan took it and turned it into a screenplay, really changing it around. That was my first lesson, at the age of sixteen, of just what happens to a writer. This was a story that I had worked pretty hard on. I remember I was driving with Bryan and we were on an off-ramp on Route 1, getting onto the highway. I was sitting in the car and I had the story in my lap. We'd had a big argument about it, and I took the entire story and threw it out the window – the only copy of it that existed, handwritten. It had been made into a script, it had

evolved. I realized right then and there that once you write it, somebody else makes it and you have to be ready for those changes to take place. So from very early on I knew I could trust Bryan to make the film that he was going to make. I couldn't expect him to make the film that I was going to make because I don't know what kind of film I would make if I were a director. And I'm not particularly worried about becoming one.

How did you two end up collaborating on Public Access?
Well, after high school I went to Australia and worked at a boarding school for nine months. I was fired. Then I hitchhiked for three months, came home, knocked around for about a month and then immediately started working for this detective agency, where I ended up staying for four years.

What did you do for the detective agency?
Well, the 'detective agency' was actually a glorified security-guard position. I think in the four years I worked there I did about six investigations, during one of which I wrecked my car. It sounds great, though: 'Yeah, I worked in a detective agency.' The biggest thing we did was security for this movie theater in Sayerville, New Jersey: the Amboy Multiplex. This was a *rough* theater. When *New Jack City* came out, Sayerville was one of four cities – along with Los Angeles, Chicago, and New York – where rioting occurred. There were constant fights, people trying to kill each other. So on the one hand, I got to play cop, and on the other, I got to watch audiences. I learned to watch movies from the audience's point of view. We were always trying to gauge which movie would have the biggest opening weekend, so that we could prepare for it securitywise. A few times we were completely wrong, like when *Tougher than Leather* came out. We thought it was going to be another *New Jack City*, and it died. But then *Exorcist 3* came out and the place exploded – fights breaking out everywhere.

Anyway, after four years of that I decided it was time to move to California to try screenwriting – Bryan was already living there. And then I was offered my own agency in Florida. I was twenty-two years old, and was being given this opportunity to run my own business. So I called Bryan and he said, 'Listen, I'd love to have you out here but there's nothing going on; you should probably go to Florida.' So I told them I would do it. I bought a new car, I bought all these clothes and then, out of nowhere, it fell through. I was left in the lurch. I had this car, I had to pay bills, I couldn't just come out to California to knock around. So I applied for the New York Police Department. I took the test with my friend J.B. and we both passed. As we were gearing up to do that, Bryan called. He had made a short film called *Lion's Den*, with Ethan Hawke – it was basically a film about a group of us from school – and we tried to make a feature-length film out of it. The script was horrible. My parts of it were written by hand. So Bryan called me and said that these people had seen *Lion's Den* and really liked it and had asked to see another script. And he made up a three-second pitch off the top of his head, which evolved into *Public Access*. It would be about a bunch of college students who start a public-access cable show in a small town, and while doing so they uncover some dirty politics in the town: a stock thriller. He asked me if I wanted to write it. And I said, sure. He said, 'Okay, I need it in fifteen days.' So I bought this shitty little Panasonic word processor – I didn't know how to type – and I wrote a draft in fifteen days. At the beginning, we had tried to write a film that would be sellable, that somebody would pick up. Bryan then got Michael Dougan involved in the writing, and he came in and took this basically glorified episode of *Murder, She Wrote* and really darkened it up. I took a look at his rewrite and was like, 'Oh, you mean I can be *dark* with it . . .' So it became more and more surreal and removed and bizarre. Bryan and I realized finally one afternoon that this was the one time in our lives we would have the chance to do whatever we wanted to do without being held responsible. We just went bananas. *Public Access* was a series of very well-placed disasters. In so many different ways, that film shouldn't have, couldn't have, wouldn't have ever gotten made, finished, and into Sundance where it won the Grand Jury prize and got us the recognition that then made *Suspects* at least more of a viable commodity.

Themewise, they're very different films. Public Access *is much more of a cultural critique and is more cynical in that regard. Do you see similarities between the two?*
Well, in both films, the bad guy gets away. Also, the 'bad guy' is not necessarily evil, just messed up – in the case of Wiley Pritcher

in *Public Access*, he's had Americana poured into him through a very strange filter. I remember that we were very angry when we wrote *Public Access* – I was becoming more and more politically aware, and it didn't hurt that Bush was in office. The film reflects that; there's a lot of anger in that movie.

So tell me how The Usual Suspects *came to be written.*
Well, it kind of came together in bits and pieces. I had been at Sundance in '93 and I was standing in line with my friend Dylan Kussmann at the theater, waiting to go into *Public Access*. He asked me what the next project was going to be, and I said that I had just recently seen a column in *Spy* magazine called 'The Usual Suspects', and I thought that would be a neat title for a movie. He wanted to know what the movie would be about and I said, 'Well, it's called *The Usual Suspects*, so I guess it's about a bunch of criminals who meet in a police lineup.' And then we stood there and designed a poster for it. I said, 'Okay, in this poster you got five guys standing in a lineup, and they're all sort of conveying their attitudes: one guy is like, "I don't want to be here", and the other guy's like, "All of you can go to hell . . ."' and Dylan interrupts me and says, 'That's the tag line.' So we decided the poster's copy would be '*The Usual Suspects:* All of You Can Go to Hell.' And we thought it was great and mentioned it to Bryan and then completely forgot about it.

About a month later, Bryan was in Tokyo with *Public Access* at the Tokyo Sundance Festival. He called to say that the people he'd been talking to who had expressed interest in working with us wanted to spend something in the neighborhood of three million dollars – could I write a film for that? I thought about it, and said, 'Yeah, I guess,' and he said, 'Well, what about that "Usual Suspects" thing you were telling me about? Can you do that?' and I said, 'Yeah, why not? At least we've got a poster.' He said he'd be home in a week and he wanted me to pitch it to him then. I had no idea what I was going to write. I was working in a law firm in downtown LA, and I was smoking at the time. I went into the break room one afternoon to have a cigarette and was sort of doodling on a piece of paper – coming up with names for characters, really racking my brain. Right in the middle of sitting in this dingy white room with a table and two chairs, I realized it looked kind of like an interrogation room. I was just running through dialogue, trying to find something that caught, and I came up with this character who was being interrogated, who was babbling – he had diarrhea of the mouth. As I was doing this, I looked up, and there was a bulletin board on the wall. I started to pull words off the bulletin board just to come up with stuff. And I started calling this guy in my head 'Verbal' because he was talking so much. The name of the office manager of the law firm was Dave Kujan, and I decided to throw his name in as Verbal's interrogator; I figured I'd think up another name later. I noticed the bulletin board was made by a company called Quartet in Skokie, Illinois, and I started to spin a little tale about being in a barbershop quartet in Skokie, Illinois.

And then the idea hit me that this is what the guy, Verbal, is going to do in the film. A few days later, I was introduced by my boss at the time to a lawyer at the firm, and she said, 'This is Keyser Sume.' The first thing I said to him was, 'You have a really cool name. You're going to be the villain in a film some day.' And he was like, 'Yeah, okay, great.' He was a very nice guy, very unassuming – much like Verbal in that he didn't really fit the name. From that point on, I began to pull names from other attorneys at the firm for the characters: there was a Fred Fenster, a Jeff Rabin. One of the guys I worked with was named Oscar, so he became Oscar Whitehead. The story really came together much in the way Verbal made it up. I just was pulling ideas from my environment.

Did you have your pitch for Bryan a week later?
The pitch I had for him was this: There's a guy being interrogated by another guy who is looking for a criminal. He's sitting in a big messy office with lots of crap in it. And there's this bulletin board on the wall. At the end of the film, when the guy who's doing the interrogating finally turns around and looks at the bulletin board after the other guy has left, he realizes that not only is this guy the guy he's been looking for, but he's made up his entire story from the board. And Bryan said, 'That's great, go with that.' And we just began hammering it out that way.

This was late 1993?
This was the Spring of '93, right after Sundance. As the story

started to develop, we had to get permission to use all of the names. It was very funny – I was at the production office and I had a conference call with Keyser Sume and Dave Kujan, and we're all talking and Keyser said – he was very polite about it – 'I'm sure you guys are going to be very successful, and I'm sure your film's going to be great, but I'd like to read the script and see how the name is presented so it won't prevent me from getting clients.' I said, 'He's not really a character; he's kind of a myth' – I'm trying so hard to soft-sell this – and he goes, 'Well, send me the script.' I was really confident when I hung up that we'd get his permission. We'd all fallen in love with the name. Anyway, I opened the script to the page where he kills his entire family. And I closed it and said, 'Bryan, we've got to change the name.' I never even sent him the script. We were all joking, imagining if the film were successful: this poor guy would walk into court one day and it would be like saying, 'Presenting the case for the defense is Darth Vader.' So then we had to figure out what we would change the name to.

How did you come up with Söze as the surname?
We knew we wanted to keep some part of the name – either Keyser or Sume. We were more partial to Keyser, obviously because of its double meaning. We were coming up with alternate names for the Devil. There are thousands of them, but Bryan hated all of them. My room-mate at the time was this sort of bizarre little collector of all sorts of strange things and he happened to have an English-to-Turkish dictionary. We went into the book and I asked him to look up 'devil', 'evil', 'fire', 'slippery' – every single metaphor we could come up with – and finally I just said, 'Look up "verbal"'. And it was *Söze.*

Are there any precedents for the character of Verbal/Keyser? He's got to be one of the most evil characters in cinema.
In the first place, I don't think he's evil. I'm not a big believer in evil in the conventional sense. I believe that he's a bad guy, an unsavory character, but my feeling is that he had no choice but to do what he did, given the life that he had assumed. Given his upbringing, his personal code, he really believed that the only way to protect his family was to kill them. Death was a more honorable way out. His children and his wife had already been ruined,

scarred for life. Previous to that event, I could see Keyser regarding his life as sort of idyllic. That while he was probably a drug dealer, or some kind of really filthy criminal, he came home at night to his beautiful wife and children and that elevated and legitimized him, sort of exonerated him from what he did. And then once that had been tampered with . . .

It's the flip side of the Batman legend.

Well, the biggest inspiration for the character of Keyser was a guy named John List. In the late '50s, early '60s, he was living in a very nice house in a very nice part of New Jersey. One day someone found his entire family – three children, his wife and his mother-in-law, I believe – murdered and rolled up into carpets and stacked in the living room. He vanished for seventeen years; just disappeared. And finally, *America's Most Wanted* did a piece on him, and shortly thereafter he was caught. Amazingly, he had the same job, and had done nothing to change his appearance. He had gotten remarried and had been this upstanding citizen. He was quiet, kept to himself and had never killed again. And I don't believe ever would. A friend of mine asked me, 'Why do you think he did that?' So I kind of thought about it for a while. On the program, they talked about his life in New Jersey and how he was, I believe, an accountant who made a lot of money but lived way beyond his means. His wife had champagne tastes, and they had this big house and these cars, and the kids were going to great private schools. When they investigated him after the murders, they realized he had gone bankrupt. So my guess was that he didn't want his family to experience poverty. They were all going to be broke, they were going to be ruined. I think that in some twisted way, he really felt like he was saving his family a lot of misery by killing them. And when they finally prosecuted him, that was his defense: that he was being merciful to his family.

So that really sort of stuck in my craw. I had the idea for a character who murders his own family long before this script ever existed. He's put in a situation where someone's going to kill his family, so he does it instead. And it's a lot quicker and a lot less painful. And of course, with Keyser, it destroys him. His family was all he had, and now he is this utterly ruthless shell of a man. I really believe that you're not born that ruthless and that evil and that cunning and that cold: you're made that way. And I think that an incident like that could make him that way. It's not that he hates anybody in particular – he's mad at life, life really screwed him. Ultimately, like every other character in the script, he really brought it on himself. He's gotten mixed up in a bad business. And everybody in the script, I think – whether they indicate it or not – understands from the beginning that this is the business they've chosen. They don't blame Keyser for killing them, that's just the way it works.

I'd like to talk about the structure of the script a bit, especially the constant shifting between past and present. This could have been handled in so many different ways: for instance, it could have simply been a two-character play.

The impetus for the structure was that, when I sat down to write the script, I had a story but I had no idea where to start. I really didn't know how to approach it. I also set a limit for myself – ten pages a day – and I had wasted a lot of the first day trying to come up with something and I needed pages. Other writers whom I've spoken with work in hours, four hours a day, eight hours a day. I'll work ten pages a day. If it takes me three minutes to cut ten pages out of another script and stick it in, that's a day's work. If it takes me fourteen hours to write twenty pages and cut it down to ten, then I'll do it that way. Anyway, I needed my pages that day and I had really just slacked. I was working on this old crappy computer at the time, and I was digging through all these old files when I found a scene that I'd probably written a year before; it ultimately became the opening scene of the film. I'd set up these elements in a scene where a guy lights a fire and another guy pisses on it and puts it out, and then the guy comes over and says, 'Are you ready?' and the other guy says, 'What time is it?' and then BANG, he's dead. It was about five pages long. I said to myself, 'Great, I'm five pages into this script.' And that really set the tone for the structure. The only change I made in the scene was lowering the camera angle, so you couldn't see the gunman. And now it became an investigation into who this guy was.

And then I decided to incorporate flashbacks. I remember going to a meeting, and the guy I was speaking with said, 'You used flashbacks in your script – that's so bold.' I never went to film school; nobody ever told me I couldn't do that. I just did it because I started with this scene and, since it took place at the end of the story, I would have to use flashbacks. When they're used to manipulate the story, I think they're fine. When they're used to salvage the story, you have a problem. There's a ton of information to digest in this script – you're never once given a break – and using flashbacks seemed like the best way to get it across.

Early on, I realized that the problem with this kind of film is, when you ask a question in the first act of the film the audience will immediately begin working on the answer; audiences are incredibly sophisticated in that way, whether they know it or not – they're very aware of formulas. For instance, Bryan and I were watching a film called *Malice*, with Alec Baldwin and Nicole Kidman. One of the reasons I think it didn't work is that there's a scene in which a girl who's later going to be a victim of this unknown rapist – the red herring of the film – is talking to Bill Pullman in his office at a university. As she turns around to leave, he bumps into this janitor. You see him in the frame for about three seconds; he just looks like an extra in a scene. The problem is, the janitor is played by the albino actor from *The Firm*. He's also in the opening scene of *In the Line of Fire*, as the counterfeiter. You see this guy in this bit part and you're like, 'Oh, *he's* the rapist, and now an hour of my life has been wasted.' Audiences are not stupid: they're going to think, 'Why is that actor whom I've seen playing the villain in other movies playing an extra's part? He's going to figure in at some point.'

So one of the things that I didn't want to do was to ask the question directly: I needed another question. And that's where the whole thing about Keaton being dead or alive came in.

Using the villain as the narrator was another good way of throwing the audience off track.

I don't know how calculated that was; the narration seemed necessary because there was so much dialogue. Verbal's narration began to just bleed over into scenes so we wouldn't have to sit there and watch him talk so much. It really was a thing where I wanted the audience to sincerely believe him, and an audience almost always believes the narrator.

One of the greatest conceits of the film is how it presents the perfect

metaphor for creating a story. In the end, the character of Verbal is doing exactly what you did in devising the fiction. Speaking of casting the least likely actor in the red herring role, I understand that you wrote the part of Verbal with Kevin Spacey in mind.
Kevin had seen *Public Access* and said he was very interested in working with us. I had actually written parts for him in other scripts. So when he expressed interest, I thought, 'All right, now how do I hold him to that? How do I make a character interesting enough for a Tony Award-winning actor to want to play him?' Again, audiences are very smart. If you'd put the biggest actor in the movie in the role of Verbal, the audience would be thinking, 'When is Dustin Hoffman going to stop limping?' Kevin, who is a very gifted actor, was not the guy you would expect to suddenly be the villain, especially at that stage in his career. We live in an age where villains' parts are handed to Jeremy Irons and Alan Rickman. We wanted to take that away from the audience. We wanted to make sure that they thought that Verbal was just a narrator.

When you were writing this, how did you establish a rhythm of cutting between past and present, interrogation and action?
It was just very intuitive. Like I said, I never went to film school so I never learned how to sell a script, and I think that's one of the strengths of this screenplay. A scene would go on for a while and I'd think, 'I've said everything I want to say and now it's boring, get out of it.' I wanted to avoid the *Saturday Night Live* syndrome, where you have a concept – a funny joke – that takes thirty seconds to execute. If you make a four-minute sketch out of it, it's not funny anymore. When a scene started to get boring, I would back up two lines and cut out of it. And you've always got the interrogation, which is the skeleton of the whole thing, with two characters, neither of whom is an idiot, creating constant conflict. When it becomes a little too saturated or a little too boring or a little too where-the-hell-is-this-conflict-going? you cut back to the story on these five cool guys who are also each involved in a different sort of conflict. And then you bring in the lawyer and you're just slowly unlayering things so that in every scene, whenever we go back to the suspects, we're off in another direction. Those are the kinds of movies that I like.

Speaking of movies you like, you mentioned The Taking of Pelham 123, *the 1974 film about the hijacking of a subway train, as being an influence.*
That movie was very successful, but nobody's ever heard of it. If you're just laying around the house on Sunday afternoons, you know if you turn on the TV it will be the featured movie.

Did you draw anything from the hijacker character played by Robert Shaw for Verbal/Keyser? They are both amoral characters with very strong wills. I think of the last scene, in particular, where Shaw's character, rather than facing trial, calmly places his foot on the third rail, electrocuting himself.
Yeah. The concept of death not being a concern to these characters. These are guys who understand fully that they'll get knocked off. It's the way they get knocked off that they won't accept. *Pelham*, to me, is the original *Die Hard*. What I love is that the movie focuses on a very smart cop and a very smart criminal: who's going to win? You want them both to win. There's a part of us that wants to see the bad guy get away, that wants to see this guy outsmart authority, and beat the system. That to me is when a movie is really good: when no one is an idiot. Early on in the development of the *Suspects* script someone asked me why Kujan was chasing this guy Keaton. What does he care? Did Keaton kill his partner? No, he's just passionate about his job. You don't have to be Vincent van Gogh to be passionate about what you do. That's a big element in films nowadays: Arnold Schwarzenegger can't just be doing the right thing, they had to kill his partner or kidnap his daughter. So many movies use revenge as motivation for characters. But I think that, unless you're analyzing the mind-set itself, it's a bad motivation. I think it's much more fascinating when a guy like Keyser is saying, 'My ass is in a sling. Here's a guy that can finger me. I gotta get rid of this guy. But I'm determined to do it without coming out, without stepping into the open.' There is an element of calculation. But still, some things are beyond his control – the sketch, for example. I didn't want to go so far as to make him *super*human. I had to be careful.

Let's talk about this film's relationship to these other crime films. While fitting very comfortably into the genre, it also tends to amplify some of its standard elements. For instance, the whole male-bonding thing is really pushed to the limits here, resulting in some very homoerotic moments – It's very homoerotic in the script.

Was this something you were deliberately trying to push the envelope on? I have a lot of gay friends and so there's a lot of gay humor floating around; there's always just a lot of that sort of imagery going on in our conversations. A lot of it was subconscious. One of the few things from the script that didn't make it into the film was part of the scene that takes place after they've hit New York's Finest Taxi Service. As it's written, they're all drinking beers. McManus says, 'My boy with the plan!' to Verbal, and they all start pouring their beers on him. The white foam from the beer is pouring all over Verbal – they're just foaming all over him – as he's being accepted by these men.

Anyway, a lot of this stuff became apparent afterwards. Hockney, for instance, is one of the more homoerotic characters in the story. When we were redubbing Verbal's voiceover introducing his character – 'Todd Hockney, without a doubt the one guy who didn't give a fuck about anybody' – we thought about having Kevin Spacey say instead, 'Todd Hockney, without a doubt a closet homosexual', because, when you watch the film through that prism, he's such a flamer. Everything is just 'cocksucker, cocksucker'. The thing about 'I'll fuck your father in the shower.' 'I live in Queens.' It just went on and on and on.

Another common trait of this type of film is the frequency of scatological references. But again, here it's almost a litany.
Well, you know, a lot of the dialogue comes from the guys I worked with as a security guard. One in particular really had a knack for these little colloquialisms; he always had an interesting slang term for everything. I wanted to put them all in there. Bryan really toned a lot of the language down in the film because it got out of hand. The script I wrote immediately after this one had, I think, two profanities in the whole script, and very little killing. It's the world I'm writing about – just because the characters speak a certain way doesn't mean that I do. These are guys who are just a bunch of disgusting, seedy people who talk in a disgusting, seedy way. In the next script we're working on, the characters are aristocrats, and they don't talk that way.

It seemed that if one character talks that way, he becomes the foul-mouthed comic-relief guy. If they all talk that way, it's different. These characters have to bond somewhere, and although they're all very different, with different conflicts, at their core, they're all the same: they're just guys. And when guys get together, whether it's to pull off a heist or just to play a game of poker, it always gets ugly, and it always comes down to the guy's sexuality. And it always comes down to that one orifice.

Let's talk about your writing style. I was intrigued by the fact that, in your directions, you introduced characters in a very terse manner, similar to something you would read on a police blotter: name, age, brief physical description. Was that conscious, or do you always write scripts that way?
To me, it's always important to keep it simple. I have a great deal of difficulty keeping track of characters and locations. My thing is to concentrate on the name, make the name interesting, and give an age if it comes in handy. In terms of giving a description, unless it's a character like Verbal, where the description is extraordinarily important, don't even bother with it. Also, I really don't believe in taking a moment out to speak to the reader. I've read scripts where the paragraph stops to describe a woman and at the end it's like, 'In a word, "va-va-va-voom".' If it's a serious scene, you've ruined that scene. You've suddenly moved away from the narrative and taken a very bad opportunity to make a very bad joke. It's very arduous reading a script: it's stale, it's boring, it's dull. The best scripts in the world clunk along. My desire is to make those paragraphs a little more interesting to read, especially when studio readers have to read them.

I know you have an extremely close working relationship with Bryan Singer. On Public Access, *he shared a screenwriting credit with you. To what extent was he involved here?*
It was always a thing that was written for Bryan to direct. Basically, the way we work is, an idea will come up, whether it's my idea or Bryan's idea, and I'll just go off and write it out. We always start with an ending, so we always know where the story is going; knowing, however, never to stay married to it. I've stayed married to endings before and it's been disastrous. You've got to let the story take its own course. So I will go off and write, then I'll bring it back to Bryan and he'll read it and say, 'Change this,

like this' – he'll put his taste into it. Then I'll go back and I'll write it again. As I'm writing, I'll come up with changes and I'll run those changes past Bryan. The best way I can describe our writing relationship is, he's directing the film from the moment it hits the drawing board. We also have our core group of people whose opinions we trust: there's Ken Kokin [co-producer of *Suspects*], and John Ottman, the editor and composer. Bryan and I always say that the film is written three times – once on paper, once on film and once on the flatbed. John, however blasphemous this sounds, has a better sense of comprehension than any of us. He's the only guy who can get away with telling me what I'm thinking. So anyway, we have these friends we turn to for input, but it always comes back to Bryan and me sitting down to hash it out.

The version of the script we're publishing here was your final draft. Is it what you sent out to potential financers?
Yeah, we sent this version to everybody. The first people we went to were the financers of *Public Access*. They were Japanese, and were very into that film, and very hands-off during production. So we brought them this script, which was much less difficult, and they didn't want anything to do with it. To this day, I don't know what it was. Actually, a lot of people didn't know what to do with it. They would get the script and then dawdle for the longest time. Their instinct was to say no, I think. After the film had been made, a woman in development at 20th Century-Fox asked me why I hadn't brought them the script. And I said, 'Well, there's no hero or villain until the last page. There's no sex, and the woman dies. The hero dies. The villain gets away and there's very little action and a lot of talking. And it's completely black.' And she said, 'All right, from a development standpoint I can see how we never would have bought it.'

So anyway, there was a producer, Robert Jones, who saw *Public Access* at Sundance, and he approached Ken, who walked him through to Bryan. I was in the process of writing the script, and Bryan told him the title and he was very interested. When he saw the script, he loved it, and he pushed to get everything done. Ultimately what happened was that Polygram and Spelling International agreed to pick up the tab for the film. And the budget of three million that we'd shot for came in at about seven. Bryan actually brought it in almost a million under budget.

And that's when you started casting?
Yeah. That was the hardest part of the film, the big nightmare. Spacey was the first person to read the script, and he committed almost immediately and was very patient through this whole process of getting the film financed. I think the script was done in August or September of '93, and the film wasn't up and going until June of '94. We didn't close a deal until December of '93. Spacey was very patient – it's my understanding that he turned down a lot of work. All the actors were called upon to be extraordinarily patient, to the point where they all committed with no guarantee of money. They all showed a great deal of faith and a great deal of loyalty. A lot of them worked for very little money. One actor worked for less money than a grip, I think.

Anyway, the casting became an issue because we were now financed directly by distributors, so we were dealing with that kind of mentality: these actors have domestic value, these actors have foreign value, we want one of these. They were giving us lists of names – 'If you can, get at least one actor off this list.' I mean, we were making offers to Tommy Lee Jones on the weekend he won his Oscar. And all this time we had this group of actors already assembled who believed in what we were doing. It became a matter of knocking heads for a very long time.

So you were very involved in casting.
Yeah. Naturally, Bryan made the final decisions, but when it came to casting certain roles, he didn't know names. So what I did was more or less weed out the people we didn't want, and come up with other people he wasn't familiar with. Francine Maisler, the casting director, and I worked very closely together. She was fantastic, the greatest. We were right in line with the exception of, I think, two characters – she didn't agree with one of mine and I didn't agree with one of hers. We both got our way. She got the actor she wanted, I got the actor I wanted. They know who they are. Once we began casting, we quickly came up with the actors that would be perfect. Chazz Palminteri, for instance, we went to first, and he didn't think he'd be able to do it. He had too many conflicts and too many things going on. Kujan became an

incredibly difficult part to cast. Then Chazz's schedule opened up for two weeks and he was in.

Were you on the set at all during production?
Bryan and I have an agreement: At 7 a.m. on the first day of shooting, it's not my script anymore. I trust Bryan; I wouldn't know how to direct a film. Of course, there were days when I came to the set and saw things going on, like that scene in the garage where Hockney and McManus sort of flirt around with each other, and I thought it was a lot of posturing, a lot of bullshit. I didn't say anything, I just left. And then I saw the scene cut together, and I was like, 'Oh. Okay.'

Let's talk a bit about some of the differences between this final draft of yours and the finished film. In the screenplay, the first time we're introduced to Verbal, it's in the form of a voiceover. In the film, he's shown delivering the same dialogue on the stand, under a very hot, white light.
We went back and forth on that. What that did was help to bridge another scene that's missing in the film: his deposition, when the two lawyers are arguing over his sentence off-screen and he's reacting to them. It gives us a sense that he's *told* this story to someone. His statement is floating around Rabin's office; everyone's talking about it. What statement? Where did he make this? And with one succinct image, you reference it.

Why was that other scene, where he's basically reacting to the two lawyers off-screen, cut? Too much information?
The script timed too long. It ran, I think, 2:12. My thing was, just make them talk faster. Turn it into Mamet (no aspersions on David Mamet, I think he's a god). After I finished the script, I was really exhausted – we had gone through a lot of rewrites and preparation – so I took a vacation. I was in a hotel in New Jersey and Bryan called and said, 'We've got to cut it.' And I thought the script was tight, as tight as we were ever going to make it. I've since learned that it can always be tighter. What ended up happening was that we had to cut out the part of Captain Leo. This was probably the saddest moment for me, because we were going to cast an actor friend of mine as Rabin, and Dan Hedaya was going to play Captain Leo. But because a lot of the cuts had

to happen in the beginning, I ended up amalgamating the two characters. Instead of having those whole scenes where Kujan's talking with Leo, sort of explaining and carefully setting up the film, it ended up being one page of Kujan and Rabin running down the hallway into the office to meet Verbal. While it seems like a scary thing to cut out an entire character, it ultimately served the film, because it established, without ever having to show a ticking clock or anything, that these people didn't have a lot of time. There was no leisure time, no sitting around the office, no witty banter with the Captain.

Also, Leo serves a pretty traditional role in this version: he's always presenting these obstacles Kujan is going to have to get over to get to the next stage of the interrogation.
He's the bullshit angry police guy. He was very standard. Leo, to me, represented the line between the authority that was protecting Verbal and the cops who were trying to do their job. I tried to make him smart enough so that he didn't seem like a foil, but there were smarter characters still. In a way, I'm glad the character was cut; he was the most clichéd part of the script.

What about the establishing scene at the restaurant with Edie Finneran and Dean Keaton? You get a real sense from that about their relationship and its relationship to his past.
It's all explained on the steps outside the police station. It's all there, who she is, what's she doing, what she's done for him, how much she loves him. And that there is a duality to Keaton. When that scene in the restaurant stays in, Keaton becomes a contradictory character rather than a dual character. He becomes a character who's like, 'Ah, I love you', and then in the next scene somebody punches him in the face and he's suddenly looking at these five suspects and thinking about changing his life again. While I totally believe that everything that happened to Keaton that night was enough for him to say, 'Enough of this shit', I also felt that there needed to be more – in this case, less. There had to be a great duality to his character.

There's a great line in the screenplay that wasn't in the film, where he says, 'I swore I'd live above myself.'
That is a line I miss, but I think in the way the scene works, it

wasn't the best solution. That is really one of my favorite moments in the film, certainly one of my favorite Gabriel Byrne moments. Keaton is so frustrated that this is happening again, and Gabriel's tone of voice says all of that when he says, 'No killing?' and Verbal says, 'Not if we do it my way.' It's a better line to end it on. I do love that original line, though. It's actually something I said drunk at a bar one evening, so it has great personal meaning, but it doesn't serve the scene, it kills the end of it. It's the same old thing: You go to the punch line, back up two lines, and cut it there.

The lineup scene, the back-to-back interrogation scenes, and the cell-block scene all have modified dialogue, and I got the sense this had to do with the actors' personalities.
That was Bryan's instinct. Fenster switches a bunch of lines with McManus. Before we'd cast, McManus was the angry, hot-headed hotshot: again, much more of a standard character. When Steven Baldwin came into the picture, McManus became much cooler, just more of a steely guy. Also, Fenster was a radically different character in the script. Here, he's older than McManus, and I wanted that quirky dynamic: the young guy protecting the older one. Like a weird father-son twist to their relationship. When Benicio del Toro took the part – a performance he fashioned from basically nothing – things changed. So Bryan took the scene in the jail cell and fudged it around – cutting into it about a page later – so that the first line that McManus says in the scene is, 'I heard you were dead.' One, it's a heavy line that immediately focuses you on McManus. And it also drives that line home. It really makes us aware. It sets up the big red herring in the story, which is that Keaton was supposedly dead and now is alive again. A lot of the changes like that had to do with the casting.

In the film, there are a couple of shots of planes landing to connect scenes taking place in different locations. One occurs when Kujan arrives in LA, and the other takes place when the five suspects go to LA to meet Redfoot. Neither of these was in the script; were they a function of trying to lessen the amount of expository information?
Partly, but we also were having a lot of problems with people being confused by where the hell these guys were. The audience is so busy digesting big chunks of information that it tends to miss a

lot of the little things. We had a group of people come in and watch an early cut of the film. And in that scene before they go to LA, McManus says he's going to go to Los Angeles and see Redfoot. Then Keaton says something about LA being a good place to lay low for a while. Then Verbal's voiceover is something about McManus's fence in LA being called Redfoot. And people were like, 'Wait. Where are they now?' You say it three times in about a minute and people don't get it because there's so much going on. So we changed the voiceover a little bit and added the shot of the plane. We wanted to avoid title cards at all costs.

That relates to another question I had, actually. In the script, your slug lines always indicate whether the scene is taking place in the present or the past. Were you confident that the temporal differences would be obvious enough in the film to avoid having to use dates in most cases?
We ourselves had a hard time keeping track of what exactly the time frame was, over how many days the story had taken place, how time jumps around and gets so mixed up. We wanted audiences to know that this was happening present-tense, and that the film opens with what had just happened the day before. So the three places we used cards were at the beginning: 'San Pedro, last night', before the first scene in New York: 'New York, six weeks ago', and when the film cuts to Giancarlo Esposito at the docks: 'San Pedro, present day'. I mean, there was no distinct landmark in San Pedro to let people know where we were; there was no 'San Pedro archway' or anything in the background, and for things like that we really had to make it clear. Again, when you're reading, you can go back and double-check everything. When you're watching a film, it's different. If you forgot where you were, you'd forget when it was happening, and if you forgot when a particular scene was happening, the movie would just be a mess and the payoff wouldn't work. We wanted to take people along for the ride.

The film really takes risks regarding Verbal's double identity when, in one of those early interrogation scenes, Verbal, fumbling, actually tries to light a cigarette. That definitely wasn't in the script.
That was added on set. Bryan really, really flirted with danger on a few things. He's very mischievous that way. The thing with the lighter was saying, on the one hand, that it couldn't have been him

lighting the cigarette on the deck of the boat, but on the other hand, it was making such a show out of the cigarette that I was afraid the audience was going to get the clue. There's another scene in the film where Verbal is sort of turned away from Kujan, and he smiles. He literally cracks a smile and lets on that he knows something. When I saw it the first time, I was like, 'What is this?!' Every time I watch the film, I'm convinced the audience has just gotten it. I can feel them all around me, getting it. Bryan does a few of those in the movie.

The directions for Verbal in the script tend to put you off track more than the film. There is one scene in which he finally mentions Kobayashi, and in the script, you have him 'blurting' the name, then 'looking around wildly'. In the film, he delivers the line with a look of absolute premeditation, being almost flirtatious about it.
Well, again, as the character changed and developed, and Kevin Spacey came in and began to give him life, he became smarter, and it doesn't serve the film, as a film, that Verbal is dumb. In the script, Verbal's presented as a dummy. I didn't want the reader to suspect for a second that Verbal knew anything. In the film he's got something going on, and it's okay that the audience knows that; it makes him more fascinating. In fact, you're so busy trying to figure out what it is he knows, you don't stop to think about who he is. It was a very good instinct on Bryan's and on Kevin's part

There is an extended scene in the script in which Verbal comes to pitch the Taxi Service scam to Keaton and has words with Edie. She also makes a statement about how hard she's worked to give Dean Keaton a second chance.
In that scene in the film, Gabriel Byrne eradicates the need for all of that with a turn of his head. As he's sitting down on the steps talking to Verbal, he looks off into the apartment somewhere and you know, immediately, what he's looking at. That's all you need, just a glance at his other life. We liked the idea that Edie was, as the story developed, less of a character and more of a representation of Keaton's other life. In the film, there's always glass, or some other barrier, between them. He's up on that little walkway looking down on her, or she's on the other side of the glass wall with Kobayashi. Edie represents the life that's been taken away from him. It became less and less necessary to

establish Edie as this character he loved. In robbing the audience of that emotion, we build on Keaton's duality.

As far as I can tell, there's only one significant incidence of scenes being shifted. During the scene in which Kujan describes Keaton's supposed death to Verbal in the script, there's a quick cutaway to Leo and Rabin listening in on the wiretap. The scene then resumes. In the film, the cutaway is replaced by a much longer hospital sequence – which occurs later in the script – before going back to the end of the scene. Was that just an editing choice?

That was a very long scene that needed to be broken up, and that was a great way to do it. Chazz's monologue just goes on and on and on; poor Chazz is given just about every word of exposition in this script. It just became a thing where there was so much talk in that little room, we had to get out for a while.

The central scene of Söze killing his family: was that something that you had always envisioned as being slightly out of focus, slightly distorted, as it is in the film? Your directions don't indicate it being treated any differently.

Well, for one, I didn't want to draw attention to the fact that I was necessarily trying to hide his identity, and two, I said to Bryan, 'This is your problem. Shoot it however you want to.' I give all the credit to Bryan in that respect. I wrote it as plainly and simply as I could, knowing that when it came time to shoot the film you would have to show a brutal, violent scene, bringing all that violence and potency to it without ever showing the character it's happening to. I never knew how Bryan was going to do it, and I don't envy him for having to figure out how.

In that last scene on the boat, one of the major 'characters' in your script, is the crane which ends up crippling Keaton. What happened to it in the film? Was it a logistical problem?

The entire sequence was written with a pier I had pictured in my head. On location, it became very different. It was a logistical nightmare to have that crane and the explosions and everything else we had going on. Also, we all agreed that it was a big telegraph to where the scene was going.

What about the final line in the film? It's a repeat of an earlier comment of Verbal's: 'And just like that, he's gone.'

That was all editing. I think it's fantastic. When we wrote the script, I hadn't been thinking of the 'round up the usual suspects' line from *Casablanca*, but as the film started to come together, *Casablanca* began to be more of an influence. Also, Dr Lecter was always being mentioned as a character similar to Keyser Söze. The endings of both *The Silence of the Lambs* and *Casablanca* utilized a crane shot with the people walking away. Intentional or not, I always saw it in my mind that way: Kujan standing in the middle of the street, lost in a mob of people, as the car is driving away behind him. And after having used the voice montage in those last few minutes, you had to end on the most powerful line. When I saw it, I was blown away.

Your script seems a lot more raw than the film. Here's one passage from your directions in that final scene on the ship: '[McManus] screams like a lunatic, shooting everything in his path, killing some men with his bare hands, shooting others, stabbing still others with a knife he has brought along.'
When I wrote the script, I was really figuring on a budget of three million dollars, assuming that Kevin Spacey would be the one guy we could get and that the rest of the cast would be made up of our friends. I saw it as being a bit brutal and a bit raw and exploitative. I was given free rein to do whatever I wanted and to have fun with it. Frankly, it's not what I prefer to see in a movie, although there are times when it's done right, when it's fun. It was to make the read interesting, to just suck you into it. I couldn't say, 'This shot will be really cool.' We didn't have the visuals there so I had to describe action and the only thing going on at that point was the violence.

How do you feel about the finished film?
Bryan and I always joke that the only way we would ever really know whether this film is any good or not would be to have our minds erased, then go in and sit down and see if it held up to our scrutiny. I don't know if the movie would get me. I don't know if I would fall for it or not.

This interview originally appeared in Scenario *magazine, which also published the script.*

The Usual Suspects

The Usual Suspects premièred at the 1995 Sundance Film Festival. The cast and crew includes:

MICHAEL MCMANUS	Stephen Baldwin
DEAN KEATON	Gabriel Byrne
DAVE KUJAN	Chazz Palminteri
TODD HOCKNEY	Kevin Pollack
KOBAYASHI	Pete Postlethwaite
VERBAL KINT	Kevin Spacey
EDIE FINNERAN	Suzy Amis
FRED FENSTER	Benicio del Toro
JACK BAER	Giancarlo Esposito
JEFF RABIN	Dan Hedaya

Casting	Francine Maisler
Production Designer	Howard Cummings
Costume Design	Louise Mingenbach
Director of Photography	Newton Thomas Sigel
Editor	John Ottman
Music	John Ottman
Co-Producer	Kenneth Kokin
Executive Producers	Robert Jones
	Hans Brockman
	François Duplat
	Art Horan
Produced by	Bryan Singer
	Michael McDonnell
Written by	Christopher McQuarrie
Directed by	Bryan Singer

A Polygram Filmed Entertainment and Spelling Films International presentation of a Blue Parrot/Bad Hat Harry production.

BLACK

The lonely sound of a buoy bell in the distance. Water slapping against a smooth flat surface in rhythm. The creaking of wood.

Off in the very far distance, one can make out the sound of sirens.

Suddenly, a single match ignites and invades the darkness. It quivers for a moment. A dimly lit hand brings the rest of the pack to the match. A plume of yellow-white flame flares and illuminates the battered face of Dean Keaton, age forty. His salty gray hair is wet and matted. His face drips with water or sweat. A large cut runs the length of his face from the corner of his eyes to his chin. It bleeds freely. An unlit cigarette hangs in the corner of his mouth.

In the half-light we can make out that he is on the deck of a large boat. A yacht, perhaps, or a small freighter. He sits with his back against the front bulkhead of the wheelhouse. His legs are twisted at odd, almost impossible angles. He looks down.

A thin trail of liquid runs past his feet and off into the darkness. Keaton lights the cigarette on the burning pack of matches before throwing them into the liquid.

The liquid ignites with a poof.

The flame runs up the stream, gaining in speed and intensity. It begins to ripple and rumble as it runs down the deck towards the stern.

EXT. BOAT – NIGHT – STERN

A stack of oil drums rests on the stern. They are stacked on a pallet with ropes at each corner that attach it to a huge crane on the dock. One of the barrels has been punctured at its base. Gasoline trickles freely from the hole.

The flame is racing now toward the barrels. Keaton smiles weakly to himself.

The flame is within a few yards of the barrels when another stream of liquid splashes onto the gas. The flame fizzles out pitifully with a hiss.

Two feet straddle the flame. A stream of urine flows onto the deck from between them.

The sound of a fly zipping. Follow the feet as they move over to where Keaton rests at the wheelhouse.

Crane up to the waist of the unknown man. He pulls a pack of cigarettes out of one pocket and a strange antique lighter from the other. It is gold, with a clasp that folds down over the flint. The man flicks up the clasp with his thumb and strikes it with his index finger. It is a fluid motion, somewhat showy.

Keaton looks up at the man. A look of realization crosses his face. It is followed by frustration, anger and, finally, resignation.

VOICE
(*off-screen*)

How are you, Keaton?

KEATON

I'd have to say my spine was broken, *Keyser*.

He spits out the name like it was poison.

The man puts the lighter back in his pocket and reaches under his jacket. He produces a stainless .38 revolver.

VOICE
(*off-screen*)

Ready?

KEATON

What time is it?

The hand with the gun turns over, turning the gold watch on its wrist upward.

The sound of sirens is closer now. Headed this way.

VOICE
(*off-screen*)

Twelve-thirty.

Keaton grimaces bitterly and nods. He turns his head away and takes another drag.

The hand with the gun waits long enough for Keaton to enjoy his last drag before pulling the trigger.

Gunshot.

The sound of Keaton's body slumping onto the deck.

Move out across the deck toward the stern. Below is the stream of gasoline, still flowing freely .

The sound of the gasoline igniting. The flame runs in front of us toward the barrels, finally leaping up in a circle around the drums, burning the wood of the pallet and licking the spouting stream as it pours from the hole.

Move out across the dock, away from the boat.

The pier to which the boat is moored is littered with dead bodies. Twenty or more men have been shot to pieces and lie scattered everywhere in what can only be the aftermath of a fierce firefight.

A crane comes into view: A huge loader for hoisting cargo on to waiting ships. The faint hum of its diesel engine grows slightly louder.

At the base of the crane is a tangle of cables and girders giving life and stability to the crane. The mesh of steel and rubber leaves a dark and open cocoon beneath the base of the crane.

Move into the darkness.

Sirens are close now. Almost here. The sound of fire raging out of control.

Sirens blaring. Tires squealing. Car doors opening. Feet pounding the pavement.

Move further, slower, into the darkness.

Voices yelling. New light flickering in the surrounding darkness.

Suddenly, an explosion.

Then silence. Total blackness.

We hear the voice of Roger 'Verbal' Kint, whom we will soon meet.

VERBAL

(*voice-over*)

New York – six weeks ago. A truck loaded with stripped gun parts got jacked outside of Queens. The driver didn't see anybody, but somebody fucked up. He heard a voice. Sometimes, that's all you need.

BOOM:

INT. DARK APARTMENT – DAY – NEW YORK – *SIX WEEKS PRIOR TO PRESENT DAY*

The black explodes with the opening of a door into a dark room. Outside, the hall is filled with blinding white light. Shadows in the shapes of men flood into the room. We can make out men in hoods with flashlights. They are laden with weapons.

VOICES

POLICE. SEARCH WARRANT. DON'T MOVE.

There is a blur of violent action and sound. Beams of flashlights cut the darkness in all directions.

Finally: A dozen flashlights land on one man. He lies naked in bed, emerging from a deep sleep. He squints at the flood of blinding white light, more annoyed than frightened. He nearly laughs at the sound of countless guns cocking. He is Michael McManus, age twenty-eight.

VOICE

(*off-screen*)

Michael McManus?

MCMANUS

Yeah.

VOICE

(*off-screen*)

Police. We have a warrant for your arrest.

MCMANUS

Will they be serving coffee downtown?

Two dozen black-gloved hands grab him and yank him out of bed.

INT. HARDWARE STORE – DAY

Todd Hockney, a dark, portly man in his thirties, stands behind the counter ringing up a customer. Several others stand in line.

Hockney finishes with the first customer and turns to the second. This customer carries no items. He looks at Hockney with a steely, concentrated stare. The five customers behind him, all men in suits, watch closely.

HOCKNEY

Can I help you?

Hockney's voice is gruff and distinctly Long Island.

CUSTOMER #1

Todd Hockney?

HOCKNEY

Who are you?

All six customers instantly produce guns and aim them at Hockney.

CUSTOMER #2

Police.

HOCKNEY

We don't do gun repair.

EXT. STREET – NEW YORK – DAY

Fred Fenster, a tall, thin man in his thirties, strolls casually down the street. He is dressed conspicuously in a loud suit and tie with shoes that have no hope of matching. He smokes a cigarette and chews gum at the same time.

He happens to glance over his shoulder and notice a brown Ford sedan with four men in it cruising along the curb. He picks up his step a little. The Ford keeps up.

He looks ahead at the corner. He tries to look as comfortable as he can, checking his watch as though remembering an appointment he is late for. The Ford stays right on him.

Suddenly, he bolts. He gets no more than a few yards before cars pour out of every conceivable nook and cranny. Brakes are squealing, radios squawking, guns cocking. Fenster is surrounded instantly. He stops short and flaps his hands on his thighs in defeat.

FENSTER

Ahh, come on.

INT. LA LANTERNA RESTAURANT – DAY

An attractive man and woman walk quickly through the front of a small New York café. They are charged with nervous, excited energy.

The man is Dean Keaton, a well-dressed, sturdy looking man in his forties with slightly graying hair. He looks much better than he did in the opening scene. The woman with him is Edie Finneran, age thirty-three, poised and attractive – easily the calmer of the two.

At the back of the restaurant they come to a staircase leading down to a dark room. Edie takes Keaton's arm and stops him.

EDIE

Let me look at you.

Keaton is uncomfortable in his suit, or perhaps the situation. Still, he smiles with genuine warmth.

Edie straightens his tie and picks microscopic imperfections from his lapel.

Now, remember, this is another kind of business. They don't earn your respect. You owe it to *them*. Don't stare them down but don't look away, either. Confidence. They are fools not to trust you. That's the attitude.

KEATON

I'm having a stroke.

EDIE

You've come far. You're a good man. I love you.

Keaton blinks then stammers, looking for a response.

Pause.

Live with it.

She kisses him and runs down the steps with Keaton close behind. Keaton playfully grabs her ass and she nearly stumbles down the stairs.

INT. RESTAURANT – DOWNSTAIRS

They come to the bottom of the steps, giggling and jabbing each other. Once off the stairs, they instantly transform as though hit with cold air. They assume a cool, professional exterior and walk two feet apart. One would look at them and see only two business associates here to ply their trade.

They walk across the dimly lit dining room to a table in the far corner where two men are already seated. The first is Stephen Yule, age fifty-five, the other is Anthony Summers, age sixty. Both men are impeccably dressed with a distinguished air. They stand and smile.

SUMMERS

Edie, nice to see you.

EDIE

Sorry we're late.

YULE

Nonsense. Sit, please.

SUMMERS

You must be Mr Keaton.

EDIE

I'm sorry. Dean Keaton –

Summers's hand is already out.

SUMMERS

Anthony Summers. Pleased to meet you.

They shake hands. Keaton takes Yule's hand next.

YULE

Stephen Yule. My pleasure.

Everyone sits at the table. All faces are smiling.

LOW ANGLE: UNDER TABLE

Edie's hand reaches out and finds Keaton's leg. Her hand runs high up his inner thigh and squeezes firmly.

Her face is absolutely calm, giving no hint of what her hand is doing. Keaton smiles and clears his throat.

KEATON

Shall we begin?

EXT. LA LANTERNA RESTAURANT

A blue Ford sedan pulls up in front of the restaurant. Five very serious-looking men in suits get out and walk inside. In the lead is Special Agent David Kujan (Pronounced Koo-yahn), *US Customs, thirtyish, dark-haired and determined.*

INT. RESTAURANT – UPSTAIRS

The five men fan out and scan the tables carefully. One of them walks up to the hostess and produces a badge.

INT. RESTAURANT – DOWNSTAIRS

YULE

Edie brought us your proposal and I'll be honest. We're very impressed. A bit skeptical, I must admit, but impressed.

KEATON

Skeptical.

SUMMERS

The concept is brilliant, we agree. But New York is hard on new restaurants. We want to be sure you'll have staying power. If we're going to give you this much money, how can we be sure we'll see our money come back long term?

Keaton looks at Edie and smiles confidently.

KEATON

It's simple, gentlemen, design versatility. A restaurant that can change with taste without losing the overall aesthetic. Our atmosphere won't be painted on the walls.

SUMMERS

This was the part of the proposal that intrigued us, but I'm not sure I follow.

KEATON

Let's say, for example –

VOICE

(off-screen)

This I had to see myself.

Keaton looks up. He sees David Kujan. Behind him are the very serious-looking guys in suits.

Keaton is not happy to see them.

KEATON

Dave. I'm in a meeting.

KUJAN

Time for another one.

KEATON

This is my attorney, Edie Finneran.

(gesturing)

This is Anthony Summers and Stephen Yule from Manhattan Trust. Everyone, this is David Kujan.

KUJAN

Special Agent Kujan. US Customs.

(Gestures to the men behind him.)

These gentlemen are with the New York Police Department. You look great, Keaton. Better than I would have thought.

SUMMERS

Is there a problem, Mr Keaton?

KUJAN

The small matter of a stolen truckload of guns that wound up on a boat to Ireland last night.

Summers's and Yule's confusion is giving way to suspicion.

YULE

Mr Keaton?

KEATON

If you will excuse us for a moment, gentlemen.

KUJAN

We need to ask you some questions downtown. You'll be quite a while.

Summers starts to get up.

SUMMERS

We should leave you to discuss whatever this is.

KEATON

Please. Sit.

Keaton stands up and throws a wad of money on the table to cover the check. He looks at Edie. She moves to stand, but he sits her back down with a hand on her shoulder.

Enjoy the meal.

(*to Edie*)

I'll call you.

Kujan takes him by the arm, but Keaton yanks away.

He looks out over the dozens of other faces in the restaurant. Everyone is looking at him with some level of surprise. If Keaton is humiliated by the whole affair, he hides it well.

INT. HALLWAY – NIGHT

Follow a pair of feet as they shuffle across the cement floor. The shoes are shabby and worn, as are the wrinkled pants that hang too low and loose at the cuffs. The right foot is turned slightly inward and falls with a hard limp. It is clear that the knee does not extend fully.

The sound of a steel door opening. The bottom corner of a steel cage comes into view. Another set of feet falls into step with the first. Another steel door and another set of feet. Another door, another and another. Five pairs of feet walk single file down the hall.

The lame feet are in the front of the line. They come to another steel door, this one solid and covered with dents and rivets.

Crane up to reveal: Roger Kint, 'Verbal' to his few friends. He has a deeply lined face, making his thirty-odd years a good guess at best. From his twisted left hand, we can see that he suffers from a slight but not debilitating palsy. Behind him are Dean Keaton, Fred Fenster, Mike McManus and Todd Hockney.

A police officer steps into the frame and opens the steel door.

Verbal steps through the door, followed by the rest.

VERBAL
(*voice-over*)
It didn't make sense that I be there. I mean, these guys were hard-core hijackers, but there I was. I wasn't scared, I knew I hadn't done anything they could do me for. Besides, it was fun. I got to make like I was notorious.

INT. LINEUP ROOM

The five men are ushered into the room in front of a white wall painted with horizontal blue stripes. Each has a number at either end to denote the height of the man in front of it. Between these lines are thinner blue lines to tell the specific height in inches.

Bright lights shine on all of them. They squint, eyes adjusting.

Keaton leans forward a bit and looks at the men in line with him. He shares a look of familiarity with Fenster and then McManus. Hockney smiles at all of them.

MCMANUS
(*to Keaton*)
Where you been, man?

VOICE
(*off-screen*)
SHUT UP IN THERE. All right, you all know the drill. When your number is called, step forward and repeat the phrase you've been given. Understand?

The men all nod.

VOICE

(*off-screen*)

Number one. Step forward.

Hockney takes a step forward. He looks directly into a mirror on the other side of the room. It is three feet square and we can make out faint light behind it. It is a two-way. He speaks in a complete deadpan.

HOCKNEY

Hand-me-the-keys, you-fucking-cocksucker.

VOICE

(*off-screen*)

Number two. Step forward.

McManus steps up and makes a gun with his thumb and forefinger. He mocks criminal intensity, pointing at the mirror. He camps up his line.

MCMANUS

Give me the keys, you motherfucking, cocksucking pile of shit, or I'll rip off your –

VOICE

(*off-screen*)

KNOCK IT OFF. Get back in line.

McManus steps back.

The other men do their bit as Verbal speaks.

VERBAL

(*voice-over*)

It was bullshit. The whole rap was a set-up. Everything is the cops' fault. You don't put guys like that in a room together. Who knows what can happen?

INT. INTERROGATION ROOM – NIGHT

Mike McManus sits in a chair in front of a white wall. He smiles at someone off-screen.

VERBAL

(*voice-over*)

They drilled us all night. Somebody was pissed about that

6'0"

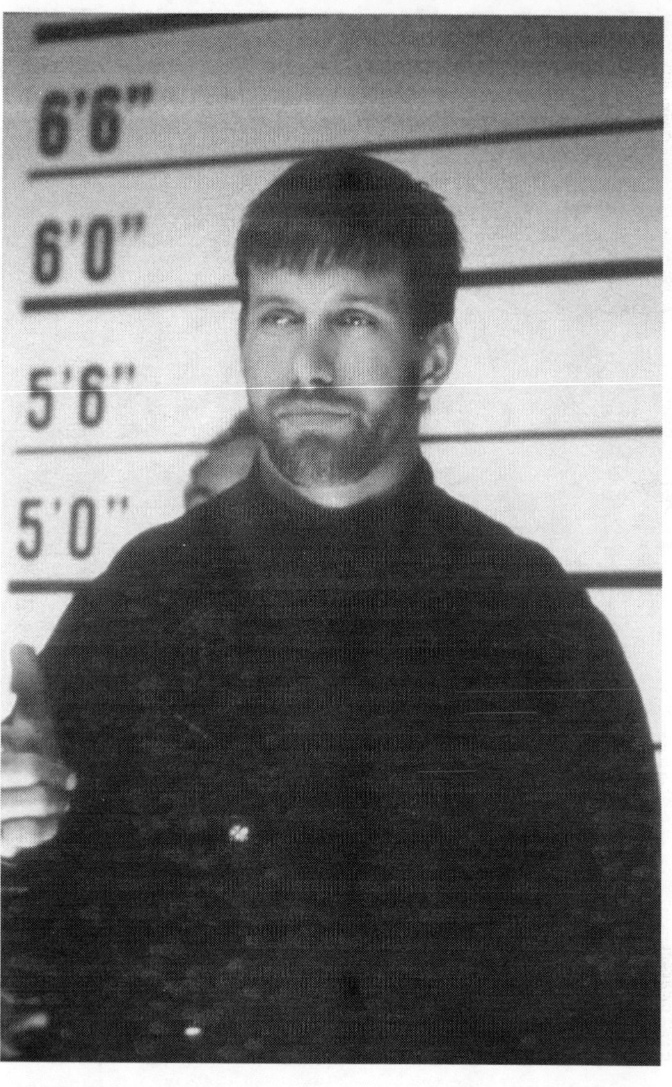
6'6"
6'0"
5'6"
5'0"

truck getting knocked off and the cops had nothing. They were hoping somebody would slip. Give them something to go on. They knew we wouldn't fight it because they knew how to lean on us. They'd been doing it forever. Our rights went right out the window. It was a violation. I mean, disgraceful.

McManus chats casually and laughs at his own jokes.

VERBAL
(*voice-over*)
They went after McManus first. He was a good guy. Crazy, though. A top-notch entry man.

VOICE
(*off-screen*)
So where'd you dump the truck?

MCMANUS
What truck?

VOICE
(*off-screen*)
The truck with the guns, fucko.

MCMANUS

You kill me, you really do. Where's my phone call?

VOICE

(*off-screen*)

Right here. Suck it out.

MCMANUS

Clever guy.

VOICE

(*off-screen*)

You want to know what your buddy Fenster told us?

MCMANUS

Do I look stupid enough to fall for that? Jesus Christ. Beat me if you gotta, but no more of the candyland tactics, man.

VOICE

(*off-screen*)

WHERE'S THE FUCKING TRUCK?

INT. INTERROGATION ROOM

Now Fenster is in the seat. He sweats profusely.

FENSTER

I don't know about any truck. I was in Connecticut all night on Friday. I want to call my lawyer.

VOICE

(*off-screen*)

That's not what McManus said.

VERBAL

(*voice-over*)

Fenster always worked with McManus. He was a real tight-ass, but when it came to the job, he was right on. Smart guy. A gofer. Got whatever you needed for next to nothing.

FENSTER

You guys got nothing on me. Where's your probable cause?

VOICE

(*off-screen*)

You're a known hijacker. You're sweating like a guilty motherfucker. That's my P.C. Save us the time. Tell us where the truck is.

Fenster knocks on the table.

FENSTER

HELLO? Can you hear me in the back? P.C.

He looks under his chair.

Where is it? I'm lookin'. It's not happening. What's going on with that? I want –

INT. INTERROGATION ROOM

Hockney's turn in the chair. He laughs it all off.

HOCKNEY

– my lawyer. I'll have your badge, cocksucker.

VERBAL

(*voice-over*)

Hockney was just a bad bastard. Pure and simple. Mean as a snake when it mattered.

VOICE

(*off-screen*)

You think so, tough guy? I can put you in Queens the day of the hijacking.

HOCKNEY

I live in Queens. What the fuck is this? You come into my store and lock me up in front of my customers. What the hell is wrong with this country? Are you guys gonna charge me or what?

VOICE

(*off-screen*)

You know what happens if you do another turn in the joint?

HOCKNEY

I'll fuck your father in the shower. Charge me, dickhead.

INT. INTERROGATION ROOM

Now Keaton sits in the chair, cool and indifferent.

VERBAL
(*voice-over*)
Keaton was the real prize for them, for obvious reasons.

VOICE
(*off-screen*)
I'll charge you when I'm ready.

KEATON
With what?

VOICE
(*off-screen*)
You know damn well, dead man.

KEATON
Hey, that was your mistake, not mine. Did you ever think to *ask* me? I've been walking around with the same face, same name – I'm a businessman, fellas.

VOICE
(*off-screen*)
What's that? The restaurant business? Not anymore. From now on you're in the getting-fucked-by-us business. I'm gonna make you famous, cocksucker.

Keaton shows just a flicker of contempt. The threat has hit home.

KEATON
Like I said. It was all your mistake. Charge me with it and I'll beat it. Let's get back to the truck.

A fist flies into the frame and connects with Keaton's jaw. His head snaps back, blood flowing freely from his mouth.

INT. CELL BLOCK

The iron door slams, locking Keaton in. He sits on the edge of the steel bed on the wall. His shirt is torn and stained with blood. His face is puffy and bruised. He looks down through the other four cells next to his.

Hockney, Fenster, McManus and Verbal all look at one another from their respective cells. They try to smile to Keaton.

VERBAL
(*voice-over*)
They sweat us all night. Came up with nothing. People don't think the cops do shit like that, but it happens all the time. And you wonder why we do what we do.

HOCKNEY
Anybody want to screw?

All five men laugh.

INT. CELL BLOCK – LATER

MCMANUS
Somebody should do something. What is this shit – getting hauled in every five minutes?

FENSTER
There's no probable cause.

HOCKNEY
Hazard of the trade, boys.

MCMANUS
What fucking trade? Okay, so I did a little time –

FENSTER
A lot of time.

MCMANUS
Shut up. So I did some time. Does that mean I get nailed every time a truck finds its way off the planet?

FENSTER
No P.C.

MCMANUS
You're fuckin'-A right, no P.C. Well, screw P.C. No right. No goddamn right. You do some time, they never let you go. Treat me like a criminal, I'll end up a criminal.

HOCKNEY

You *are* a criminal.

MCMANUS

Why you gotta go and do that? I'm trying to make a point.

KEATON

Then make it. Christ, you're making me tired all over.

McManus spins around and looks at Keaton, sitting on the edge of the bed, looking away.

MCMANUS

I heard you were dead.

KEATON

You heard right

HOCKNEY

The word *I* got is you hung up your spurs, man. What's that all about?

MCMANUS

What's this?

HOCKNEY

Rumor has it, Keaton's gone straight – cleaning house. I hear he's tapping Edie Finneran.

FENSTER

Who's that?

HOCKNEY

She's a heavyweight criminal lawyer from uptown. Big-time connected. She could erase *Dillinger*'s record if she tried. I hear she's Keaton's meal ticket.

(*to Keaton*)

Is it true?

MCMANUS

How about it, Keaton? You a lawyer's wife? What sort of 'retainer' you giving her?

Keaton shoots McManus a fiery glare.

FENSTER

I'd say you've gotten on his main and central nerve.

KEATON

Do your friend a favor, Fenster, keep him quiet.

FENSTER

You're clean, Keaton? Say it ain't so. Was it you that hit that truck?

MCMANUS

Forget him. It's not important. I was trying to make a point.

KEATON

(*ignoring McManus*)

This whole thing was a shakedown.

FENSTER

What makes you say that?

KEATON

How many times have you been in a lineup, Fenster? It's always you and four dummies. The P.D. pays homeless guys ten bucks a head half the time. No way they'd line five felons in the same row. No way. And what the hell is a voice lineup? A public defender could get you off of that.

MCMANUS

Can I finish what I was saying?

FENSTER

So why the hell was I hauled in and cavity searched tonight?

KEATON

It was the Feds. A truckload of guns gets snagged, Customs comes down on NYPD for some answers – they come up with us. They're grabbin' at straws. It's politics – nothing you can do.

FENSTER

I had a guy's fingers in my asshole tonight.

MCMANUS

Is it Friday already?

FENSTER

Fuck you. I'll never shit right again. So who did it? Own up.

KEATON

I don't want to know.

MCMANUS

Nobody asked you, working man. Now what I was *trying* to say –

HOCKNEY

Fuck who did it. What I want to know is, who's the gimp?

All eyes suddenly turn on Verbal. He has been quietly listening the whole time without uttering a word.

KEATON

He's all right.

HOCKNEY

How do I know that? How about it, pretzel-man? What's your story?

KEATON

His name is Verbal Kint. I thought you guys knew him.

MCMANUS

Verbal?

VERBAL

Roger, really. People say I talk too much.

KEATON

We've met once or twice. Last time was in . . .

VERBAL

County. I was in for fraud.

KEATON

You were waiting for a lineup then, too. What happened with that?

VERBAL

Ninety days, suspended. I walked.

HOCKNEY

So you did it?

VERBAL

To your mother's ass.

Verbal looks away from Hockney, awaiting a violent response. Everyone slowly starts to laugh. Hockney looks as if he is about to boil in his own skin.

KEATON

(*to Hockney*)

Let it go.

Verbal smiles at Keaton appreciatively.

MCMANUS

AS I WAS SAYING. We've all been put out by this; I figure we owe it to ourselves to salvage a little dignity. Now, Fenster and I got wind of a possible job –

KEATON

Why don't you just calm down?

HOCKNEY

What do you care what he says?

MCMANUS

Yeah, I'm just talking here, and Hockney seems to want to hear me out. *I know* Fenster is with me –

(*to Verbal*)

How about you, guy?

VERBAL

I'm interested, sure.

MCMANUS

There, so you see, I'm going to exercise my right to free assembly.

McManus taps the bars of his cell and the others laugh.

KEATON

I'm not kidding. Shut your mouth.

MCMANUS

You're missing the point.

KEATON

No, *you're* missing the point. Shut up. I don't want to hear anything you have to say. I don't want to know about your 'job'. Just don't let me hear you. I want nothing to do with any of you –

(*beat*)

I beg your pardon, but all of you can go to hell.

HOCKNEY

Dean Keaton, gone the high road. What is the world coming to?

MCMANUS

Forget him, then.

(*whispering*)

Now, I can't talk about this here in any detail, but listen up.

Everyone but Keaton gravitates toward McManus's cell as he begins to speak in low, hushed tones.

VERBAL

(*voice-over*)

What the cops never figured out, and what I know now, was that these men would never break, never lie down, never bend over for anybody. Anybody.

EXT. PIER – DAY – MARINA DEL REY – *PRESENT*

It is morning in the aftermath of the opening scene.

Harsh sunlight shines on the mass of dead bodies on the dock; many of them burned beyond recognition.

Police swarm everywhere; photographers are taking pictures of the scene while a team of men in rolled-up sleeves and plastic gloves pick at the remains.

Beyond is a large firetruck on the edge of the pier. Two men operate a water cannon, dousing the smoldering remains of a burned-out ship's hull in the water.

A gray Chevy sedan pulls up to the scene. Two men in dark suits get out. The first is Special Agent Jasper Briggs of the FBI. He is tall and fit, in his late thirties. His partner is Special Agent Joel Cheever, fortyish – shorter and heavier than Briggs, with thinning hair.

A Uniform Cop trots up to them. Briggs holds up his badge.

BRIGGS

Agent Jasper Briggs, this is Agent Joel Cheever, FBI. How many dead?

COP

Fifteen so far. We're still pulling some bodies out of the water.

BRIGGS

I don't want any of the bodies moved until we've had a chance to go over this, understood?

COP

I have to clear the scene. I've got word direct from the Chief –

Briggs lights a cigarette, only half-listening.

BRIGGS
(*unimpressed*)
Yes, yes. Spooky stuff. Any survivors?

COP
Two. There's a guy in LA County Hospital, but he's in a coma. The DA has the other guy – a cripple – from New York, I think. Listen, the Chief said –

BRIGGS
Let's get to it.

Briggs and Cheever walk away from the cop, ignoring him completely. They wander through the carnage on the pier.

EXT. OCEAN

A half-mile out from the pier.

The sea is choppy, stirred by the wind. An object floats into view a few feet away, bobbing in the water.

It is a dead body – a man, face down, wearing a checkered bathrobe. He drifts quietly toward the open ocean.

INT. HEARING ROOM – DAY – LA – *PRESENT*

Verbal Kint sits in a chair in front of a microphone, his brow beaded with sweat.

On the wall behind him is the seal of the State of California.

He is cleaner, better kept, in a well-cut suit and neatly trimmed hair. He looks older than he did in New York – worn down.

A flurry of voices banter off-screen. Verbal's eyes follow the voices back and forth.

VOICE #1
(*off-screen*)
My client offers his full cooperation in these proceedings. In exchange, his testimony is to be sealed and all matters incriminating to himself are to be rendered inadmissible.

VOICE #2
(*off-screen*)
The District Attorney's office will comply, provided –

VOICE #1
(*off-screen*)
No provisions. Nothing. My client's testimony for his immunity.

VOICE #2
(*off-screen*)
May I be frank, Counselor? I suspect the political power behind your client as much as I respect it. I don't know why Mr Kint has so many faceless allies in City Hall, and I don't care. The embarrassment he helped cause the City of New York will not happen here.

VOICE #1
(*off-screen*)
Immunity.

VOICE #2
(*off-screen*)
Counselor, I *will* prosecute your client.

VOICE #1
(*off-screen*)
Then prosecute. I will be very impressed to see the District Attorney manage to bring in twenty-seven simultaneous counts of murder against one man with cerebral palsy. I would think a man with your job would agree with these alleged 'faceless people in City Hall' you mention.

VOICE #2
(*off-screen*)
One would think counsel is veiling a threat.

VOICE #1
(*off-screen*)
Counsel isn't *veiling* anything.

VOICE #2
(*off-screen*)
I'll take my chances then. I'll feel safer without a job if a man like Mr Kint is behind bars.

VOICE #1
(*off-screen*)
Mr Kint will plead guilty to weapons possession.

VOICE #2
(*off-screen*)
You're joking.

VOICE #1
(*off-screen*)
Weapons. Misdemeanor one.

VOICE #2
(*off-screen*)
Counselor, you're insulting me.

VOICE #1
(*off-screen*)
Counselor, *you're* bluffing. Shall I push for misdemeanor two?

Voices mumble off-screen. Verbal fidgets in his chair.

VOICE #2
(*off-screen*)
Misdemeanor one. Fine. This is ludicrous.

A tiny smile and a genuine look of disbelief flash across Verbal's face.

(*off-screen. Clearing throat*)
As for the rest of the charges – grand larceny, arson . . . murder – the District Attorney will accept the subject's testimony in connection with the above-mentioned events and in exchange will offer complete immunity. The transcript . . . The transcript of said testimony will be sealed and all matters incriminating to Mr Kint will be rendered inadmissible.

Verbal lets out a long-held sigh of relief.

INT. OFFICE – DAY – LOS ANGELES – *PRESENT*

Special Agent David Kujan sits in a cheaply upholstered chair next to Sergeant Jeffrey Rabin, a stocky man in his thirties with built-in angry features. The two men sit across from Captain Anthony Leo, fifty, gray-haired. He's angrier-looking than Rabin and with good reason.

LEO

This was never my problem. Why is this suddenly my problem?

KUJAN

The Customs Office would appreciate your cooperation.

LEO

(*to Rabin*)

He keeps saying that.

(*to Kujan*)

Why do you keep saying that?

KUJAN

I need some time with him.

LEO

You can't have it. I have the Governor – I'll say that again – the Governor of the State of California telling the Mayor telling the Chief telling me that he wants no part of this. Internal affairs is probing my colon every fifteen minutes to assure this guy gets due process. That little cripple in there is so politically wired up right now, I couldn't arrest him if he shot me in the ass.

KUJAN

Doesn't that seem a little –

LEO

The answer is no.

KUJAN

Twenty-seven dead bodies in the marina, 91 million dollars in cash, two drug mobs and four hijackers from New York – dead.

LEO

Hail God's wrath. Go back to New York, Agent Kujan.

KUJAN

If it was a dope deal, where is the dope? If it was a hit, who called it in?

Leo seems to cave in a bit to Kujan's logic.

LEO

What is your theory?

KUJAN

Dean Keaton was the mind behind all of this.

LEO

The dead cop?

KUJAN

The ex-cop, yes. He was a schemer. If anyone knows where the dope is, it's him. He was bounced off the force in the '70s on a bribery charge and took up hijacking and smuggling. Customs has been building a case on him for three years.

RABIN

Yeah?

KUJAN

Before he was arrested in New York, we were led to believe Keaton was dead. Killed in a warehouse fire in New Jersey.

RABIN

Okay?

KUJAN

Now I have a professional con man and habitual liar telling the District Attorney that he saw Keaton die on a boat in the marina moments before his body was burned in a fire. Am I getting through?

RABIN

You're asking us to believe –

KUJAN

– that some or all of that mess in the marina was the work of Dean Keaton and that he is still alive.

RABIN

(*skeptical*) Come on.

LEO

Really, Agent Kujan. It is a bit hokey. What about the Argentines? Could the boat have been a decoy?

KUJAN

Begging the Captain's pardon, but if there's anything I've learned as a cop, it's always the obvious solution. Nothing is that complicated in the real world.

LEO

(*to Rabin, sarcastic*)

I, of course, have yet to sample this 'real world'.

KUJAN

No offense.

LEO

Taken. My hands are tied. He has total immunity and his story checks out. He doesn't know what you want to know.

KUJAN

I don't *think* he does. Not exactly, but I think there's a lot more to Verbal Kint's story. The truth may be that he doesn't *know* there's more. I need time to talk to him and feel it out. I want to know why twenty-seven men died on that pier for what looks to be 91 million dollars worth of dope that wasn't there. Above all, I want to be sure that Dean Keaton is dead.

LEO

The Mayor doesn't care, Kujan.

KUJAN

But he does care about the embarrassment in New York.

LEO

Absolutely.

KUJAN

How embarrassed will this city be when I get to the bottom of this myself? I will, and you know it. How will the Mayor explain how someone in this city is moving four and a half tons of cocaine that vanished from under two dozen dead bodies that no one looked into? I'll see that he's made to try. You have my word on that.

Leo looks at Rabin, who has been silent all this time. Rabin shrugs indifferently. Leo looks back at Kujan.

LEO

I know you get what you want, Kujan. I've heard all about the trouble you've caused, and I know you won't hesitate to do it to me. As a cop yourself, I'm sure you can understand how little of the Academy truly applies, but a long way back in the mists of time I seem to recall someone mentioning something about the law, so I'll let you talk to him and find out what you can. The cripple makes bail in two hours, and when he posts, he's out of my hair.

KUJAN

(*pointing to Rabin*)

I need his office.

RABIN

Now hold on.

LEO

You're determined to push me.

KUJAN

Rabin here says he won't talk in an interrogation room. He's convinced they're all wired.

LEO

I can't believe this guy.

KUJAN

Thank you.

LEO

(*to Rabin*)

Go with him.

(*to Kujan*)

And if you interfere with his due process, I'll see to it you squat hard on the business end of a federal indictment.

EXT. HALLWAY

Kujan and Rabin are walking quickly down the hall.

KUJAN

I need a wire.

RABIN

You're amazing. No.

KUJAN

I need your help here. Verbal is a liar, and what's worse, he has diarrhea of the mouth. I'm going to need you to cross-check everything that he says. I don't have time to filter his bullshit.

RABIN

Fuck you.

KUJAN

No, fuck you. Politics has mired my ass since I walked through the front door of this building. As far as I'm concerned, you're part of the problem. I will get what I want from this case if I have to charge the House of Representatives with obstruction to do it.

RABIN

They warned us about you. Disruptive, unethical, impractical.

KUJAN

And?

RABIN

And a string of convictions a mile long.

KUJAN

Ninety-one million in cash –

RABIN

I know, I know. Twenty-seven dead things and the whole thing with the thing. Sure.

KUJAN

So you'll help?

RABIN

It stops when I say. I'm serious.

KUJAN

I see. You're busting my balls. We'll be friends, I suppose.

RABIN

I most sincerely hope so. Contact or cover?

KUJAN

What?

RABIN

Inside. Contact or cover?

KUJAN

You have any questions for him?

RABIN

The recipe for ice.

KUJAN

Thank you, Sergeant Cavalcade-of-Laughter. I'll take contact.

INT. HOSPITAL – DAY

A door marked INTENSIVE CARE.

The door bursts open. Suddenly, the hallway is a flurry of activity.

Dr Lisa Plumber, age fifty, walks quickly beside Jasper Briggs.

Briggs walks with all of the determination of a battalion of Chinese infantry.

Dr Alan Saccone, a young intern in his late twenties, rushes up to them.

PLUMBER

Alan, this is Special Agent Jasper Briggs from the FBI. Agent Briggs, this is Dr Alan Saccone.

SACCONE

Nice to meet you.

BRIGGS

Is he talking?

SACCONE

He regained consciousness less than an hour ago. He spoke – not English – then he lapsed.

BRIGGS

Hungarian?

SACCONE

I don't –

BRIGGS

It was Hungarian. Most of them were Hungarian. Any Hungarians from the old country on staff?

SACCONE

We have a Turkish audiologist.

Saccone opens a door and Briggs barrels through.

INT. HOSPITAL ROOM – ICU

Briggs comes to an abrupt halt at the foot of a bed surrounded by a massive tangle of medical equipment. In the center of it all is the as-yet-unnamed Arkosh Kovash, mid-thirties. His body is nearly mummified in bandages and plaster from waist to chin. One leg is badly burned and undressed except for some sort of gel smeared from mid-thigh to the ankle.

Kovash is conscious and lucid, but barely. He sees Briggs and instantly begins babbling in a tide of Hungarian.

BRIGGS

Will he die?

PLUMBER

There's a chance. He's been shot four times in the stomach, he has burns over 30 per cent of his body. There's still a bullet lodged in his back.

Briggs walks over to Kovash and kneels down on the bed beside him.

He looks closely at his battered and scalded face. He listens to him for a moment. Kovash goes on incessantly.

Briggs pulls a cellular phone out of his jacket and dials.

BRIGGS

Call hospital security and put a man on the door until the police get here.

Saccone looks at Plumber.

Move, I'm not kidding.

Saccone runs out of the room. Kovash babbles louder and louder, trying to get Briggs's attention. Briggs sticks a finger in one ear to block him out and hear the phone.

PLUMBER

Is he dangerous?

BRIGGS

Yes.

Someone picks up on the other end of the phone.

Joel, it's Briggs. I'm down at LA County. The guy they pulled out of the marina is Arkosh Kovash . . . Yes, I'm sure . . . No, he's all fucked up . . . What? I can't hear you.

(*to Kovash*)

Shut up, Hugo, I'm on the phone.

(*into phone*)

Yes . . . No . . . Not until I put someone on him. Listen, I need you to send me someone who can speak Hungarian. He's awake and talking like a Thai hooker . . . How should I know? Get me someone who can talk to him –

Briggs is suddenly distracted by something Kovash has said. In the middle of a long string of unintelligible dialect, he has spouted two words that have gotten Briggs's attention.

He turns and looks down at the tattered man in the bed. Kovash realizes Briggs is listening and says the two words again.

KOVASH

Keyser – Söze.

BRIGGS

What?

He waves his hand, gesturing for Kovash to say it again.

KOVASH

Keyser – Söze.

BRIGGS

No shit?
(*into phone*)
Joel, call Dan Metzheiser over at Justice and find Dave Kujan from Customs.

INT. WORKSHOP – DAY

Kujan stands over a workbench behind Louis Grisham, a thin, rumpled man in his thirties. Louis fiddles with an array of wires and recording devices. Rabin stands a few feet away, draining a mug of coffee.

LOUIS

How much time do I have?

KUJAN

Three minutes.

LOUIS

No way. I need a half hour.

RABIN

Stuff a mic in his pants.

LOUIS

If I don't wire him right, it could show, or malfunction. If the mic isn't right, all you'll hear is his clothes rubbing against it.

KUJAN

Do you have a small wireless?

Louis holds up a mic the size of a cigarette lighter. Kujan snatches it with one hand and grabs Rabin's coffee cup with the other in mid-sip.

Kujan tucks the mic in his palm, holding it in place with his ring and little finger. He holds the mug with his index and middle fingers. The mic is buried behind the mug in the hollow of his hand. He holds it up to Rabin and Louis. They nod approvingly.

INT. RABIN'S OFFICE – LATER

Rabin's office can only be described as a disaster area. The desk is cluttered with weeks, perhaps months or even years of paperwork that could never conceivably be sorted out.

Above his desk is a bulletin board. It is a breathtaking catastrophe of papers, wanted posters, rap-sheets, memos and Post-its. This is in the neighborhood of decades. Rabin is a man with a system so cryptic, so far beyond the comprehension of others, that he himself is most likely baffled by it.

Kujan walks in, holding the mug of coffee in one hand. In the other is a thick stack of paper. He drops it on the table.

RABIN

Verbal, this is Agent Kujan from Customs.

VERBAL

Nice to meet you.

RABIN

He wants to ask you a few questions before you go.

VERBAL

What about?

KUJAN

About Keaton mostly, but I'd like to start at the lineup back in New York.

This hits a chord. Verbal looks down at the floor.

VERBAL

Can I get a coffee?

KUJAN

In a while. What happened after the lineup?

VERBAL

I'm really thirsty. I used to dehydrate as a kid. One time it was so bad, my piss come out like snot. I'm not kidding. It was all thick and –

RABIN

All right. I'll get you a fucking coffee.

Rabin walks out of the office, slamming the door behind him.

VERBAL

That guy is tense. Tension is a killer. I used to be in a barbershop quartet in Skokie, Illinois – the baritone was this guy named Kip Diskin. Big fat guy. I mean like Orca fat. He used to get so stressed in the –

KUJAN

(*exasperated*)

Verbal, you know we're trying to help you.

VERBAL

Sure. And I appreciate that. And I want to help you, Agent Kujan. I like cops. I would have liked to have been a Fed myself but my C.P. was –

KUJAN

Verbal, I know you know something. I know you're not telling us everything.

VERBAL

I told the DA everything I know.

INT. WORKSHOP

Rabin stands over Louis at his workbench. He adjusts several dials on a receiver until the voices of Kujan and Verbal come clearly through a tinny speaker on the wall. Rabin reaches over for a nearby pot of coffee.

KUJAN
(*voice-over*)
I know you liked Keaton. I know you think he was a good man.

VERBAL
(*voice-over*)
I *know* he was good.

KUJAN
(*voice-over*)
He was a corrupt cop, Verbal.

INT. RABIN'S OFFICE

VERBAL
Sure. Fifteen years ago, but he was a good thief. Anyway, the cops wouldn't let him go legit.

KUJAN
Keaton was a piece of shit.

VERBAL
You trying to get a rise out of me?

KUJAN
I want to hear your story.

VERBAL
It's right here.

He taps a finger on the stack of paper that Kujan brought in. Kujan picks it up and thumbs through it.

KUJAN
According to your statement, you are a short-con operator. Run-of-the-mill scams. You're a textbook shyster. Everything you do, you learned from somebody else.

VERBAL
That's been suppressed. Anything in there is inadmissible.

KUJAN
Oh, I know. Hell of a lawyer you have. Expensive?

VERBAL

I'm so loaded.

(*laughs*)

I love this. I pulled down about a half-mil with those guys. It's all in there. Along with a few guys I popped – New York's Finest Taxi Service – I threw in jobs I did over the last ten years to firm up the deal. What the hell? They might as well have never happened.

KUJAN

Sweet deal. Total immunity.

VERBAL

Well, I do have the weapons charge. I'm looking at *six* whole months hard time.

KUJAN

You know a dealer named Ruby Deemer, Verbal?

VERBAL

You know a religious guy named John Paul?

KUJAN

You know Ruby is in Attica?

VERBAL

He didn't have my lawyer.

KUJAN

I know Ruby. I helped put him away. He's very big on respect. Likes me very much. His people stop by my house sometimes to send me his best.

Verbal sees this getting to something. His smile fades.

Now, I know your testimony was sealed. Ruby is well-connected. He still has people running errands for him. What do you think he'd say if he found out you dropped his name to the DA?

VERBAL

There's nothing in there about Ruby.

KUJAN

I'll be sure to mention that to him.

Verbal is not smiling anymore. He stares at Kujan with utter contempt, knowing he is being shafted.

The first thing I learned on the job, know what it was? How to spot a murderer. Let's say you arrest three guys for the same killing. Put them all in jail overnight. The next morning, whoever is sleeping is your man. If you're guilty, you know you're caught, you get some rest – let your guard down, you follow?

VERBAL

No.

KUJAN

I'll get right to the point. I'm smarter than you. I'll find out what I want to know and I'll get it from you whether you like it or not.

VERBAL

I'm not a rat.

Kujan puts his hand on the transcript of Verbal's confession. Rabin walks in with a cup of coffee. Verbal takes it with his good hand and sips it with relish.

Ahhh. Back when I was picking beans in Guatemala, we used to make fresh coffee. Right off the trees, I mean. That was good. This is shit, but hey . . .

RABIN

Can we get started again?

KUJAN

Now what happened after the lineup?

Verbal sneers at Kujan, unable to change the subject.

EXT. POLICE STATION – NEW YORK – NIGHT *SIX WEEKS PRIOR*

Keaton stops at the top of the front steps of the police station and lights a cigarette. Edie comes out behind him, fuming mad.

EDIE

. . . and the desk Sergeant is actually trying to tell me he *can't* release you? Can you believe that? You weren't even charged. New York police – Jesus. I want to take pictures of your face to bring to the DA first thing in the morning.

KEATON

Just forget about it.

He looks across the street and sees Fenster and McManus talking at a newsstand. McManus is thumbing through magazines.

EDIE

Absolutely not.

Keaton looks to his right and sees Hockney trying to hail a cab.

I'll have this thing in front of a grand jury by Monday.

KEATON

Edie, please. I don't want to hear this right now. What did Summers and Yule say?

EDIE

They want more time to think about investing.

KEATON

Goddammit.

EDIE

They just said they wanted time.

KEATON

Time for what, Edie? Time to look into me a little more, that's what. No matter how well you cover my tracks now, they'll find out who I am.

EDIE

Give me some credit. I got you this far, let's go to the grand jury. This is never going to stop if we –

KEATON

No. It's never going to stop, period. It won't take more than a week before every investor in this city is walking away from me. It's finished. I'm finished.

Just then, Verbal bumps into him on his way out the door. He excuses himself and hobbles down the steps, oblivious to whom he has bumped into as he tries to navigate the stairs.

EDIE

Don't give up on me now, Dean.

KEATON

They'll never stop.

EDIE

I love you.

KEATON

(*to himself*)

They ruined me tonight.

EDIE

Dean. I love you. Do you hear me?

Verbal gets to the sidewalk and stops. He turns, realizing it is Keaton on the steps.

Let's just go to my place. We'll worry about this tomorrow.

Keaton and Verbal look at one another for a moment. Keaton then looks over to the newsstand and sees Fenster looking at him.

KEATON

Huh?

Fenster taps McManus, who stops babbling and looks up from his magazine to see what Fenster is looking at.

EDIE

Come home with me, please. Dean?

Keaton looks at Hockney, who has one foot in a cab. He is looking at Fenster and McManus, who are looking at Keaton. This makes Hockney look up at Keaton as well.

Suddenly, Edie tunes in to what is going on. She notices the others on the street. She reaches over and takes Keaton by the arm, pulling gently. She glares at the others.

Come home, Dean.

KEATON
(*distant*)

All right.

Verbal looks at everyone else from where he stands on the street. Fenster, McManus and Hockney all look at him and then at each other. It is a strange moment of unspoken understanding.

All eyes finally turn to Keaton, high on the front steps of the police station, as he walks away with Edie.

INT. HALLWAY – NIGHT

Verbal stands in front of an apartment door. He hesitates for a long moment before he knocks.

After a moment, the door opens and Keaton stands on the other side of it. He is wearing a bathrobe and smoking a cigarette. He looks at Verbal without any expression whatsoever.

KEATON

What are you doing here? How did you find me?

VERBAL

I just asked one of the detectives downtown. He seemed pretty happy to tell me.

Keaton curses under his breath and motions for Verbal to come in.

INT. EDIE'S APARTMENT

Verbal walks in and sits down on the couch, watching Keaton cautiously. He looks around the large apartment, beautifully furnished and decorated.

Edie walks into the room in a man's button-down shirt and sweatpants.

EDIE

Dean, who was at the –

She stops when she sees Verbal. Verbal stands and smiles nervously.

VERBAL

How do you do?

KEATON

Verb – Roger, this is Edie Finneran. Edie, this is Roger Kint, he was at –

EDIE

(*cold*)

I know who he is.

VERBAL

I hope I didn't disturb you.

EDIE

I hope so, too, Mr Kint. Can I get you something to drink?

VERBAL

A glass of water would be nice.

Edie shoots a look at Keaton on her way out of the room. Keaton tries to hush his voice despite his anger.

KEATON

What the hell do you want?

VERBAL

I wanted to talk to you. The other guys –

KEATON

I did you a favor by standing up for you tonight, but don't think we're friends. I'm sorry, but I have other things –

VERBAL

They're gonna do a job. Three million dollars, maybe more.

Keaton is speechless. Verbal sits on the couch again.

They sent me to offer you a cut. We could use a fifth man, a driver – that's all you'll do.

Edie walks in with a glass of ice water and hands it to Verbal.

Thank you.

Verbal drinks slowly. Edie stands over him, her face blank. It is an awkward moment. She deliberately makes Verbal uncomfortable.

Long pause – finally:

EDIE

So what is it you do, Mr Kint?

VERBAL

Umm . . .

EDIE

A hijacker like Dean here? Or something more creative?

KEATON

That's enough, Edie.

EDIE

(*angry*)

I don't know what you came here for, but we won't have any part of it.

KEATON

Edie, please.

Keaton takes Edie by the arm and tries to guide her toward the other room. She pulls away, anger turning to rage.

EDIE

I've spent the last year of *my* life putting *his* back together again – I won't have you come in here and – What makes you think – GET OUT. GET OUT OF MY HOME. HOW DARE YOU COME HERE?

Keaton is pulling her now. She yanks her arm away and shoves him.

Don't touch me. Just don't.

She turns and walks out of the room. Somewhere in the back of the apartment, a door slams.

Keaton turns and glares at Verbal. Verbal cringes.

KEATON

Get out.

VERBAL

If you'll just let me –

Suddenly, Keaton lunges. He grabs Verbal by the lapels and lifts him off the couch, moving him effortlessly across the room and slamming him into the wall next to the front door. He opens it.

Don't hurt me.

KEATON

(*seething*)

Hurt *you*, you sonofabitch? I could – kill you.

Keaton starts to shove Verbal out the door.

VERBAL

(*quickly*)

They're going to hit the Taxi Service.

Keaton freezes. Long pause.

New York's Finest Taxi Service.

KEATON

They – that's bullshit. They don't operate anymore.

VERBAL

McManus has a friend in the 13th Precinct. They're coming out for one job. Friday night. They're picking up a guy smuggling emeralds out of South America. Fenster and McManus have a fence set to take the stuff.

KEATON

What fence? Who?

VERBAL

Some guy in California. His name is Redfoot.

KEATON

Never heard of him.

Keaton moves to throw Verbal out. Verbal grabs Keaton and holds tight.

VERBAL

You *have* to come.

KEATON

What's with you? What do you care whether I come or not?

VERBAL

They – they don't know me. You do. They won't take me unless you go. Look at me. I need this.

KEATON

Tough break.

VERBAL

Don't tell me *you* don't need this. Is this *your* place?

Keaton is unable to answer.

They're never going to stop with us, you know that. You can't go legit any more than I can. After a certain point, they *make* you a criminal. This way, we hit the cops where it hurts and get well in the meantime.

Keaton lets Verbal go and steps back, thinking.

As clean as you could ever get, they'll never let you go now.

KEATON

I don't do that anymore.

VERBAL

I've heard about you, Keaton. You can't be good and stay true to yourself. It's in your blood, same as the rest of us. I'm not knocking you. You look like you've got a good little scam going with this lawyer –

WHAM. Keaton punches Verbal in the stomach and drops him to one knee. Verbal coughs and tries to find his breath.

KEATON

You watch your mouth.

VERBAL

(*gasping*)

Okay, okay. You say it's the real thing? That's cool.

Keaton reaches for Verbal. Verbal flinches. Keaton gently helps him up and guides him to the couch. They both sit. Keaton reaches for a pack of cigarettes and lights one for each of them.

KEATON

I apologize.

Verbal takes one and has a few drags, catching his breath and rubbing his stomach in pain.

Finally:

VERBAL

I was out of line.

KEATON

You okay?

VERBAL

I'll be all right.

KEATON

Well, I'm sorry.

VERBAL

Forget it.

(*beat*)

I'll probably shit blood tonight.

Keaton laughs. Verbal thinks about it for a moment and laughs with him.

Keaton's laughter trails off. He thinks for a moment.

KEATON

How are they going to do it?

VERBAL

McManus wants to go in shooting. I said no way.

KEATON

Fenster and Hockney?

VERBAL

They're pretty pissed off. They'll do anything. Now, I got a way to do it without killing anyone, but like I said, they won't let me in without you.

KEATON

Three million?

VERBAL

Maybe more.

KEATON

No killing?

VERBAL

Not if we do it my way.

Long pause.

KEATON

(*lost in thought*)

I swore I'd live above myself.

Verbal smiles, knowing he has him.

EXT. KENNEDY AIRPORT – NIGHT

VERBAL

(*voice-over*)

New York's Finest Taxi Service was not your normal taxi service. It was a ring of corrupt cops in the NYPD that ran a high-profit racket driving smugglers and drug dealers all over the city. For a few hundred dollars a mile, you got your own black-and-white and a police escort. They even had their own business cards.

Oscar Whitehead, a tall, gray-haired man in his fifties, comes out of the international terminal in a white linen suit. He holds a large suitcase in his right hand.

After a while, somebody started asking questions and the Taxi Service shut down. Ever since then, Internal Affairs had been waiting to catch them in the act.

Oscar stands on the curb long enough to light a cigarette. After a moment, a police cruiser pulls up to him. He opens the back door and gets in.

And that was how we started. McManus came to us with the job; Fenster got the vans; Hockney supplied the hardware; I came through with how to do it so no one got killed – but Keaton – Keaton put on the finishing touch. A little 'Fuck you' from the five of us to the NYPD.

The care drives out of the airport. A green minivan follows at a distance.

INT. POLICE CAR

Sergeant Bill Strausz, a meaty, imposing-looking man in his forties, drives the car. Beside him is a thin, greasy-looking patrolman, Steve Rizzi. They are two drivers for New York's Finest Taxi Service.

RIZZI

How was the flight?

Oscar hands Rizzi a thick envelope.

OSCAR

Will that get me to the Hyatt?

Rizzi counts the stack of hundred dollar bills in the envelope.

RIZZI

That'll get you to Cape Cod.

The two men laugh. Strausz watches the road, expressionless.

EXT. HIGHWAY

The cruiser heads toward the heart of Manhattan.

EXT. STREET – LATER

The police car makes its way down a wide, abandoned street. A white minivan pulls out behind it and heads the same way.

INT. POLICE CAR

Strausz looks in the rearview mirror. The white minivan is flashing its highbeams.

STRAUSZ

What the –

RIZZI

LOOK OUT.

Strausz looks in front of him. A green minivan swerves in front of them from out of nowhere. Strausz slams on the brakes and skids to a halt. The white minivan rams them from behind.

Strausz and Rizzi are stunned for a moment as two more vans screech up on either side of the cruiser, boxing it in with only a few inches between them.

The cruiser is surrounded on all sides.

Suddenly, both side windows shatter and shotgun barrels come through. They come to rest, one on Strausz's left temple, one on Rizzi's right. Rizzi looks out of the corner of his eye. He sees the driver of the van next to him holding the shotgun with one hand. A stocking over the driver's head obscures his face.

Strausz looks straight ahead. The minivan in front of them is missing a back window. Another man with a stocking over his face aims a submachine gun at them from inside.

By the twisted right hand holding the front of the gun, we know it is Verbal.

Strausz and Rizzi raise their hands without being asked.

EXT. STREET

The driver of the white minivan gets out with a heavy blanket in one hand and a sledgehammer in the other.

Moving like lightning, he jumps on to the roof of the police car and covers the overhead lights with the blanket.

He stands on the front of the roof and swings the hammer down.

INT. POLICE CAR

SMASH: *The hammer punches three huge holes in the windshield and finally caves it in. Strausz and Rizzi are covered with pebbles of broken glass. Oscar clutches his bag in the back seat. He trembles in terror.*

The man standing on the roof doubles over and sticks a gun in Strausz's face. His face hangs upside down and, covered from the mouth up in a stocking, looks gruesome. By the voice, we know it is Mike McManus.

MCMANUS

GIVE ME THE SHIT.

STRAUSZ

Give it up.

Oscar hands the suitcase up to the front of the car and Strausz passes it to McManus.

INT. FRONT VAN

Through the front windshield, we see Keaton at the wheel. Verbal is behind him, leaning out the back window.

Beneath his stocking mask, we see Keaton is trembling and sweating, sickened by what he is doing.

He glances up at the rearview mirror and looks at the scene outside. He looks down at the floor in shame, shaking his head.

INT. POLICE CAR

MCMANUS

The money.

Strausz looks at Rizzi.

THE MONEY. LET'S HAVE IT.

Rizzi hands the money through the remains of the windshield.

McManus takes the money and stuffs it in his jacket. He steps back and pulls out a can of spray paint. He quickly starts to spray something on the roof of the car.

STRAUSZ

Do you know who I am?

A hand reaches into the window on the driver's side and rips Strausz's badge off of his shirt.

Strausz dares to turn his head right at the shotgun pointing at him through the window. On the other end is a masked and smiling Todd Hockney.

HOCKNEY

We do now, jerk-off.

McManus vanishes as quickly as he came, bolting back to his van.

Strausz and the others look straight ahead at the van in front. Verbal still trains a subgun on them.

RIZZI

Shit.

The subgun explodes in a hail of bullets. Everyone in the car screams and flails for cover.

Bullets rip through the hood of the car. Metal pops, paint and glass fly everywhere. The radiator bursts in a geyser of steam.

The four vans peel away and vanish down a side street, revealing what is left of the police car. None of the men in the car is visible.

Slowly, Strausz pokes his head up. Rizzi comes up a moment later, then Oscar. The car is destroyed, but they are unhurt.

Pause. Oscar vomits over the seat, spraying Strausz and Rizzi.

EXT. STREET – LATER

The scene is swarming with fresh police cars. Strausz and Rizzi are fielding questions from a dozen other cops. Photographers are everywhere.

The roof of the cruiser is emblazoned in huge, yellow, spray-painted letters. They read: NY'S FINEST TAXI.

VERBAL
(*voice-over*)

The *Times* got a call that night and was on the scene before the cops were. Strausz and Rizzi were indicted three days later. Within a few weeks, fifty more cops went down with them. It was beautiful. Everybody got it right in the ass, from the Chief on down.

INT. GARAGE – NIGHT

Hockney, Fenster, McManus and Verbal are all laughing in a secluded garage. They are still in their black clothes from the robbery. Hockney is throwing everyone cans of beer.

Keaton sits off by himself. He watches the others, unable to join in the festivities.

The others sit around a cheap card table. It is covered with uncut emeralds. Dozens of them. Everyone is in awe.

MCMANUS

There's more than I thought.

HOCKNEY

When does the fence come?

MCMANUS

Redfoot? He never comes to see me. I have to go see him.

VERBAL

In California?

MCMANUS

Yeah. It'll take a few days. Me and Fenster –

HOCKNEY

Hold the fuckin' phone. You and Fenster? No, no, no.

MCMANUS

Guys, come on.

HOCKNEY

I'm sure you can understand my hesitation.

FENSTER

Then who goes?

HOCKNEY

We *all* go. How about it, Keaton?

All eyes turn to Keaton. He comes out of his trance.

KEATON

We need to lay low for a while.

MCMANUS

Fine with me.

Pause.

Everyone looks at everyone else, the moment of distrust blowing over. All eyes drift back to the emeralds on the table.

Hockney begins to snicker, then McManus, then Fenster. Verbal joins in at last.

McManus grabs Verbal and hugs him, shaking him violently.

My boy with the plan.

Suddenly, everyone yells and pours beer over Verbal's head. He laughs as he is drenched in white foam, nearly choking as the others chant his name.

Keaton watches from across the room, trying in vain to smile.

INT. ELEVATOR – DAY

Keaton and Verbal ride up in silence.

VERBAL

We're going to miss the flight.

KEATON

We'll make it.

VERBAL

Don't do this. Send her a letter – something.

KEATON

We'll make it.

EXT. HALLWAY

Keaton and Verbal get off the elevator. They come out down the hall from a set of glass doors. A sign on the doors reads: MONTGOMERY AND LAGUARDIA – ATTORNEYS AT LAW.

Just inside the doors is a waiting room. Keaton grabs Verbal by the arm and stops him. He nods his head towards the doors.

Verbal looks and sees Edie walking across the waiting room to an old woman reading a magazine. The two women talk for a moment.

Keaton stands behind Verbal as if to hide behind the meek cripple. He watches Edie help the old woman up and escort her into the office. Edie is laughing with the old woman.

Keaton's face is marked with guilt and anguish.

VERBAL

She'll understand.

Verbal turns to Keaton, but he is gone. He has gotten back on the elevator. The doors begin to close. Verbal takes one last glance at Edie and turns back to Keaton.

INT. OFFICE WAITING ROOM

Edie seems to sense something behind her. She turns and looks through the glass doors and out into the hall.

The hall is empty. She goes back to chatting with the old woman.

INT. RABIN'S OFFICE – DAY – LA – *PRESENT*

KUJAN

Heartwarming. Really, I feel weepy.

VERBAL

You wanted to know what happened after the lineup, I'm telling you.

KUJAN

Oh, come on, Verbal. Who do you think you're talking to? You really expect me to believe he retired? For a woman? Bullshit. He was using her.

VERBAL

He loved her.

KUJAN

Sure. And I'm supposed to believe that hitting the Taxi Service wasn't his idea, either.

VERBAL

That was all Fenster and McManus.

KUJAN

Come on. Keaton was a cop for four years. Who else would know the Taxi Service better? That job had his name all over it.

VERBAL

Sure he knew, but Edie had him all turned around. I'm telling you straight, I swear.

INT. WORKSHOP

Rabin is listening to the conversation with Louis.

Suddenly, the door bursts open. Captain Leo stands in the hall.

LEO

WHAT THE HELL IS GOING ON HERE, RABIN?

Rabin turns without flinching and motions for him to be quiet.

This kind of shit is cleared with me. I want it shut down right now.

RABIN

Listen.

LEO

TO WHAT? YOU LISTEN TO ME.

RABIN

Cap, just listen for two minutes.

INT. RABIN'S OFFICE

VERBAL

You keep trying to lay this whole ride on Keaton. It wasn't like that.

KUJAN

Let me tell you something. I know Dean Keaton. I've been investigating him for three years. The guy I know is a cold-blooded bastard. IAD indicted him on three counts of murder *before* he was kicked off the force, so don't sell me the hooker with the heart of gold.

VERBAL

You got him wrong.

KUJAN

Do I? Keaton was under indictment a total of seven times when he was on the force. In every case, witnesses either reversed their testimony to the grand jury or died before they could testify. When they finally did nail him for fraud, he spent five years in Sing Sing. He killed three prisoners inside – one with a knife in the tailbone while he strangled him to death. Of course, I can't prove this, but I can't prove the best part, either.

Kujan pauses to drink some coffee.

Dean Keaton was dead. Did you know that? He died in a fire two years ago during an investigation into the murder of a witness who was going to testify against him. Two people saw Keaton enter a warehouse he owned just before it went up. They said he had gone in to check a leaking gas main. It blew up and took all of Dean Keaton with it. Within three months of the explosion, the two witnesses were dead – one killed himself in his car and the other fell down an open elevator shaft.

INT. WORKSHOP

Captain Leo and Rabin look at one another as they listen.

KUJAN

(*on speaker*)

Six weeks ago, I get an anonymous call telling me I can find Keaton eating at La Lanterna with his lawyer, and there he is. Now, because he never profited from his alleged death and because someone else was convicted for the murder we tried to pin on Keaton, we had to let him go.

INT. RABIN'S OFFICE

KUJAN

He was dead just long enough for a murder rap to blow over, then he had lunch.

VERBAL

I don't know about that.

KUJAN

I don't think you do. But you say you saw Keaton die. I think you're covering his ass and he's still out there somewhere. I think he was behind that whole circus at the marina. My bet is he's using you because you're stupid and you think he's your friend. You tell me he's dead, so be it. I want to make *sure* he's dead before I go back to New York.

VERBAL

(*blurting*)

He wasn't behind anything. It was the lawyer.

KUJAN

What lawyer?

Pause.

What lawyer, Verbal?

Verbal stammers for a moment, looking around wildly.

VERBAL

Back when I was in that barbershop quartet in Skokie, Illinois, I used to have –

Kujan grabs Verbal's shirt and yanks him half out of his seat.

KUJAN

You think I don't know you held out on the DA? What did you leave out of that testimony? I can be on the phone to Ruby Deemer in ten minutes.

VERBAL

The DA gave me immunity.

KUJAN

NOT FROM ME, YOU PIECE OF SHIT. THERE IS NO IMMUNITY FROM ME. You atone with me or the world you live in becomes the hell you fear in the back of your tiny mind. Every criminal I have put in prison, every cop who owes me a favor, every creeping scumbag that works the street for a living, will know the name of Verbal Kint. You'll be the lowest sort of rat, the prince of snitches, the loudest cooing stool pigeon that ever grabbed his ankles for the man. Now you talk to me, or that precious immunity they've seen so fit to grant you won't be worth the paper the contract put out on your life is printed on.

Verbal looks at Kujan with utter contempt.

VERBAL

There was a lawyer. Kobayashi.

KUJAN

Is he the one that killed Keaton?

VERBAL

No. But I'm sure Keaton's dead.

KUJAN

Convince me. Tell me every last detail.

INT. WORKSHOP

LEO

Start writing.

Rabin grabs a pad and pencil.

INT. HOSPITAL – DAY

Kovash's room is now filled with people. Jasper Briggs stands next to Daniel Metzheiser, a balding man in his forties. Next to him is Dr Plumber. Across from her is Alan Saccone.

Sitting beside the bed is Tracy Fitzgerald, a casually dressed woman in her late twenties. She holds a fifteen by twenty-inch drawing pad on her lap.

Police fill the hall. People are talking loudly outside. Lionel Bodi, a cop in his mid-twenties, pushes his way in.

BRIGGS

Are you the translator?

BODI

Patrolman Lionel Bodi, sir.

PLUMBER

Agent Briggs, I can't allow any more of this.

BRIGGS

I'll see to it we're gone before he blows his porch light, Doctor.

Briggs gestures to Tracy.

(*to Bodi*)

This is Tracy Fitzgerald. She's a composite sketch artist from County.

The two young people smile at each other nervously.

BODI

Hi.

TRACY

Hi.

METZHEISER

(*impatient*)

I've got a noon meeting, Briggs.

PLUMBER

Agent Briggs, this is out of hand.

BRIGGS

Everyone calm down.

(*to Bodi*)

Ask this man about the shoot-out at the marina.

Bodi speaks in Hungarian to Kovash. Kovash smiles with relief when he hears his own language. Kovash replies spilling over in a stream of Hungarian.

BODI

He says they were buying . . . It doesn't make sense. I'm sorry, I'm a little rusty. They were there to buy something.

BRIGGS

Dope, we know.

BODI

Not dope. Something else. Some – what? . . . He doesn't know what they were buying. But not dope . . . People.

METZHEISER

Your witness is whacked, Briggs.

BODI

He says he'll tell us everything he knows if we protect him.

BRIGGS

Tell him fine.

Bodi relays this. Kovash frantically shakes his head, babbling.

BODI

He needs guarantees. He says . . . his life is in danger . . . He has seen the Devil . . . looked him in the eye.

METZHEISER

I'll be on my way.

Briggs grabs Metzheiser by the arm.

BRIGGS

(*to Bodi*)

Tell him to tell this man what he was telling me before. Who is the Devil? Who did he see?

Bodi relays the question.

KOVASH

Keyser Söze.

Metzheiser is suddenly interested. Kovash continues.

BODI

He says he saw him in the marina. He was shooting . . . killing . . . killing many men.

METZHEISER

Did he say Keyser Söze? He *saw* Keyser Söze.

KOVASH

Keyser Söze. Keyser Söze.

BODI

He says he knows his face. He sees it when he closes his eyes.

METZHEISER

Ask him what this Devil looks like.

BRIGGS

(*to Tracy*)

Ready?

Tracy holds up her pad and pencil. She nods.

EXT. LA SKYLINE – DAY – *FIVE WEEKS PRIOR*

VERBAL

(*voice-over*)

McManus's fence was this guy named Redfoot. He had a good reputation around LA. Seemed like a good guy – Looked like a cowhide full of thumbtacks.

EXT. PARKING LOT – NIGHT

All five guys stand in an empty parking lot. It is utterly quiet.

An old but well-kept Cadillac creeps into the lot from the far end and idles up to them. The windows are tinted too much to see in. The car passes within a few feet of them and drives on.

A moment later, a chrome and leather monster of a Harley-Davidson pulls into the lot. The rider is dressed in an almost comical array of leather, silver and suede.

He waves to the Caddy as it parks a few yards from Keaton and the others. It sits quietly, almost menacing.

As he gets closer, we can see he is wearing one black boot and one red. Keaton is still looking at the boots when the bike pulls up to them and stops.

Redfoot and McManus shake hands.

REDFOOT

How've you been?

MCMANUS

Good. You?

REDFOOT

All right. How's it going, Fenster?

FENSTER

Getting by.

REDFOOT

You got it?

McManus holds up a briefcase.

Redfoot takes it and gets off the bike. He walks over to the Caddy. The door of the Caddy opens. Redfoot hands the case to someone inside we cannot see. The door closes.

KEATON

(*whispering*)

Snazzy dresser, this guy.

A moment later, the door of the Caddy opens again. Someone hands Redfoot a different briefcase and he walks back over to McManus. He hands him the case.

McManus hands the case back to Hockney. Hockney opens it, revealing the stacks of money inside.

REDFOOT

You must be Keaton.

MCMANUS

Jesus, I'm sorry. Redfoot, this is Dean Keaton, that's Todd Hockney and that's Verbal Kint.

REDFOOT

(*to Verbal*)

The man with the plan.

Verbal smiles.

Are you guys interested in more work?

McManus moves to answer, but Keaton cuts him off.

KEATON

We're on vacation.

REDFOOT

I've got a ton of work and no good people.

MCMANUS

What's the job?

Keaton shoots McManus a foul look. McManus pretends not to notice.

REDFOOT

A jeweler out of Texas named Saul. He rents a suite at a hotel downtown and does free appraisals. Buys whatever he can. Word is he moves with a lot of cash. I'll take the merchandise, you keep the green.

HOCKNEY

Security?

REDFOOT

Two bodyguards. Pretty good.

MCMANUS

Give me time to check it out?

REDFOOT

I'd expect nothing less.

MCMANUS

Tempting. We'll call you.

REDFOOT

Take your time. Enjoy LA.

KEATON

A friend of mine in New York tells me you knew Spook Hollis.

REDFOOT

I hear you did time with old Spook. Yeah, he was a good egg. I used to run a lot of dope for him. Fuckin' shame he got shivved.

KEATON

I shivved him.

Now McManus is shooting the angry look at Keaton.

Better you hear it from me now than somebody else later.

REDFOOT

Business or personal?

KEATON

A little of both.

REDFOOT

Ain't it a crime? Call if you're interested.

Redfoot fires up his bike and takes off with the Caddy close behind.

MCMANUS

(*to Keaton*)

What's your fucking problem?

KEATON

One job, that was the deal.

MCMANUS

Take it as it comes, brother.

KEATON

This is bullshit.

McManus laughs and walks away. Fenster and Hockney follow. Verbal turns to Keaton.

VERBAL

What is it, Keaton?

KEATON

(*distant*)

Something – I don't know.

(*shaking himself*)

I ever tell you about the restaurant I wanted to open?

Keaton walks off. Verbal follows him in confusion.

VERBAL

(*voice-over*)

LA was good for about two hours. We were from New York. There's no place to eat after one; you can't get a pizza that doesn't taste like a fried fruit-bat, and the broads don't want to know you if you don't look like a broad. Within a few days the last of us was ready to go back, but Keaton wouldn't have it, so he really didn't have a choice. We went to work.

INT. PARKING GARAGE – NIGHT

McManus walks along a line of cars. He comes across a black Mercedes and stops. He looks down at the license plate and walks over to the next car, a green Honda. He pulls a Slim Jim out of his jacket and pops the lock on the Honda. He reaches in, opens the hood. He walks around and sticks his head in the engine.

INT. VAN

Verbal sits behind the wheel. Keaton is beside him. Hockney and Fenster are in the back. They all watch McManus from where they are parked a few dozen yards away.

INT. PARKING GARAGE

DING DING: *The elevator bell sounds at the far end of the garage. The doors open. Two men in ill-fitting suits get out and look around cautiously. The first is Frank Tucci, a big-bellied, white-haired menace. The other is John Higham, lean and bad-skinned. They are bodyguards and give it away by their every careful move.*

They turn back to the elevator and motion to someone inside. Out walks Saul Berg, a slightly overweight man in his forties with an open-collar silk shirt and a thick gold chain on his hairy chest. He carries a large aluminum briefcase.

He lets his guards do the worrying. He walks straight to his car.

Saul passes McManus under the hood of the Honda. He takes out his keys and pushes a button on his key-chain. The Mercedes beeps three times, telling Saul his alarm is off.

Tucci keeps an eye on McManus. Higham watches Saul.

McManus pretends to tinker with the car's engine. He has put two pistols just inside the grill and keeps them within reach.

The van on the other side of the garage starts and pulls out of the spot. It cruises over toward the Mercedes.

Tucci sees the van. He and Higham are suddenly busy trying to keep track. They hear laughing behind them and turn around.

Fenster and Hockney are walking toward them. They are sporting moustaches and sunglasses in addition to matching suits, each with loud plaid sport coats, decades out of style. Saul glances at Tucci and Higham.

HIGHAM

Just get in the car, Saul.

Under the hood of the Honda and out of sight, McManus pulls on a black ski mask.

The van gets closer.

HOCKNEY

I get out of the car, and, man, if the thing wasn't wrecked. And I see this broad in the back seat with nothing on.

Saul gets in the car quickly but calmly as Fenster and Hockney laugh and talk louder. They look drunk – the desired effect.

I'm laughing so hard I can't breathe –

Tucci and Higham try to take it all in stride. Saul's reverse lights come on and he begins to back out of the spot.

And the fat guy comes out of the car with his pants on backwards and says –

BOOM: The van suddenly roars up from behind and rams into Saul's Mercedes. Hockney and Fenster drop the drunk act and snap to. They both pull out guns and start screaming.

DON'T MOVE, YOU FUCKERS.

FENSTER

RIGHT THERE. FREEZE.

Tucci and Higham throw their hands in the air. Hockney and Fenster grab them and reach into their belts to get their guns.

Keaton jumps out of the van and runs up to Saul's car, his face covered in a ski mask. He yanks on the door handle but it is locked. Saul sits in terror behind the wheel. Keaton pulls out a pistol and smashes the window with it.

KEATON

Give me the case.

Saul reaches over for the case. Keaton trains the gun on him.

Suddenly, Saul comes up with a pistol and points it at Keaton. Keaton sidesteps and grabs his wrist. The gun goes off into the fender of the Honda.

Hockney and Fenster both look over at the sound of the gun.

Tucci and Higham seize the opportunity. Tucci grabs Hockney, Higham grabs Fenster. The four men grapple for the guns.

McManus steps out from under the hood of the car with a gun in each hand. He trains a pistol on each bodyguard and takes a breath. They are some ten feet apart and moving erratically. Hockney and Fenster constantly fall in the line of fire.

McManus walks around the four men, keeping a pistol trained on each of the guards. Finally, he comes to an angle where they are all in front of him. One guard is a few feet away, the other is ten feet past him.

McManus's POV: The closer of the two moves in and out of the sights of the pistol in McManus's right hand, while the one farther away does the same with the pistol in the left.

Verbal jumps out of the van and moves toward them to help.

BOOM: *Both of McManus's guns go off like one shot. Tucci and Higham collapse, each with a bullet in his head.*

Pause.

The only sound is Saul grappling with Keaton for the gun. His arm is halfway out the window. His elbow rests in the door frame. Keaton cannot get the gun out of his hand. Finally, he pushes down with all his weight. Saul's elbow breaks backwards on the door frame. He screams in agony. The gun falls from his hand.

All five of the men look at each other for an impossibly long moment. The confusion is only aggravated by Saul's screaming.

Slowly, Keaton raises his pistol and aims it at Saul. His hand trembles, his eyes squint to near slits. His finger tenses and slacks off over and over again on the trigger.

BOOM: *Verbal shoots Saul. Keaton looks at him in surprise. Verbal trembles more than he does.*

The garage is silent.

HOCKNEY

What the hell?

MCMANUS

Bad day. Fuck it.

DING DING: *The elevator light comes on. All five men look.*

KEATON

Move.

Keaton reaches into the car and grabs Saul's case. Everyone else piles into the van. Keaton gets in as Verbal is driving for the exit.

A man and a woman come out of the elevator. They talk quietly and walk toward their car. The man notices that the Honda's hood is up.

MAN

What's that?

WOMAN

Honey?

MAN

I think someone tried to steal the car again. Christ.

He stomps over to the car to check the damage.

His wife sees a hand on the ground just behind the car. She walks around the back and finds the bodies of Tucci and Higham. She stammers, unable to speak.

The man is under the hood of the car. He looks to his left and sees Saul in the next car. His arm hangs out of the window, twisted in an odd direction, and there is a bullet hole in his ear.

Suddenly, the woman finds her voice. She screams.

INT. VAN

The mood in the van is grim. Everyone is silent. Keaton pops the clasps on the case and opens it.

KEATON

Son of a bitch.

Everyone looks in the case. It is filled with cash on one side. The other side is filled with clear plastic bags of white powder.

EXT. PARKING LOT – NIGHT

Keaton and the others walk through the empty lot. Redfoot is waiting this time. His bike is parked to one side. He sits on the fender of the dark Caddy. Keaton throws Saul's case on the ground at Redfoot's feet. Redfoot picks it up.

KEATON

What can we expect next, asshole?

REDFOOT

I know you're pissed. I can understand.

KEATON

I came here to kill you.

REDFOOT

Get a grip. I didn't know.

KEATON

You didn't know.

REDFOOT

The job got thrown to me by a lawyer from upstate.

KEATON

Who is he?

REDFOOT

He's a middleman for somebody. He doesn't say and I don't ask.

KEATON

I want to meet him.

REDFOOT

He wants to meet you. He called last night and asked me to set it up. What do I tell him?

KEATON

Tell him we'll meet. If you're lying to me, Redfoot . . .

REDFOOT

Keaton, you're a real bad-ass, but get off my tip.

Keaton lunges for Redfoot. The Caddy doors instantly pop open and rifle barrels come into view from within. Everyone grabs Keaton and holds him back.

Real shame about Saul getting whacked. Lots of cops looking for the guys that did it. I'm sure they'll get around to asking me.

Redfoot gets on his bike and starts it.

KEATON

Fuck you.

REDFOOT

I'll be in touch. Stay low.

He drives off. The Caddy waits until he is completely out of sight before following.

INT. RABIN'S OFFICE – DAY – *PRESENT*

KUJAN

So this lawyer . . .

VERBAL

Kobayashi.

KUJAN

Came from Redfoot.

VERBAL

Right.

KUJAN

And why leave this out when you talked to the DA?

A knock at the door.

Rabin sticks his head in.

RABIN

Someone to see you, Agent Kujan.

Kujan steps out into the hall, shutting the door behind him.

INT. HALLWAY

Kujan smiles instantly, recognizing the man standing with Rabin.

KUJAN

Jasper. What are you doing here?

BRIGGS

I've been looking for you all afternoon. You still after the coke that walked out of last week's bloodbath in the marina?

KUJAN

Yeah.

BRIGGS

You can stop looking. There was no coke. I've been in LA County with a guy they pulled out of a drainpipe in Del Rey two days after the shoot-out. He came to this morning and started talking. He was part of a Hungarian mob there to do a deal with a bunch of gwats from Argentina. He says it was definitely *not* a dope deal.

KUJAN

There was 91 million –

BRIGGS

We know, but our man says no way on the dope. This Hungarian tells me the whole bunch was pulling stumps for Turkey the next day. They had no time to negotiate that kind of product and no means to move it.

KUJAN

What was the money for?

BRIGGS

He didn't know. No one doing the deal knew except a few key people. This guy says they were real hush about it. Whatever it was it was highly sensitive. The mob's best people were there.

KUJAN

I don't get it.

BRIGGS

They tell me you got the cripple from New York in there. He mention Keyser Söze.

KUJAN

Who?

BRIGGS

Bear with me here.

INT. RABIN'S OFFICE – LATER

BOOM: The door bursts open.

KUJAN

Who is Keyser Söze?

Verbal looks up in shock. He drops his cigarette and trembles at the mere mention of the name.

VERBAL

Ahh, fuck.

INT. HOTEL ROOM – DAY – *TWO WEEKS PRIOR*

Keaton stands while the rest sit and listen.

KEATON

So I need to know if anyone can think of anybody. Somebody with power. Enough to possibly track us from New York.

MCMANUS

Look. We've been over it for an hour now. I say we pack up and run. Let's go back to New York. At least get out of LA.

A knock at the door.

KEATON

Here we go.

Keaton opens the door.

Mr Kobayashi, a tall, slim, well-groomed Asian stands in the hall. He has a briefcase in his hand. He smiles politely.

KOBAYASHI

Mr Keaton?

Keaton stands back and lets him in. Kobayashi looks them over.

KOBAYASHI

I am Mr Kobayashi. I've been asked by my employers to bring a proposal to you gentlemen. That must be Mr Hockney. I recognize Mr Fenster from his mugshot, as well as Mr McManus.

(*to Verbal*)

I can only assume that you are Mr Kint. I believe you were the one who disposed of Saul. My employer sends his gratitude. A most unexpected benefit.

Everyone looks at each other, shocked that he would know this.

KEATON

What can we do for you?

KOBAYASHI

My employer requires your services. One job. One day's work. Very dangerous. I don't expect all of you to live, but those who do will have 91 million dollars to divide any way they see fit.

KEATON

Who's your boss?

KOBAYASHI

My employer wishes to remain anonymous.

KEATON

Don't jerk me off. We all know what this is. You don't work with me if I work with you without knowing who I'm working for. Now let's cut the shit. Who's the man?

KOBAYASHI

I work for Keyser Söze.

A strange look crosses Keaton's face. Skepticism, mockery and just a hint of fear. Hockney, McManus and Fenster all share similar looks.

KEATON

What is this?

VERBAL

Who's Keyser Söze?

KOBAYASHI

I am sure you've heard a number of tall tales, myths and legends about Mr Söze. I can assure you, gentlemen, most of them are true.

VERBAL

Who's Keyser Söze?

KOBAYASHI

Judging by the sudden change in mood, I am sure the rest of your associates can tell you, Mr Kint. I have come with an offer directly from Mr Söze. An order, actually.

KEATON

An order.

KOBAYASHI

In 1981, Mr Keaton, you participated in the hijacking of a truck in Buffalo, New York. The cargo was raw steel. Steel that belonged to Mr Söze and was destined for Pakistan to be used in a nuclear reactor. A very profitable violation of UN law. You had no way of knowing this, because the man shipping the steel was working for Mr Söze without his knowledge. Mr Fenster and Mr McManus hijacked a two-prop cargo flight earlier this year out of Newark airport. The plane was carrying platinum and gold wiring. Also set for Pakistan.

Kobayashi turns and points at Hockney.

Two months ago, Mr Hockney stole a truck carrying gun parts through Queens –

Everyone looks at Hockney. He smiles shyly.

– guns allegedly set to be destroyed by the State of New York.

They were to be 'lost' in a weigh station and routed to Central America. Again, Mr Söze using pawns who had no knowledge. Which brings us to Mr Kint.

He turns and looks at Verbal. Verbal crumbles under his stare.

Nine months ago, one of Mr Söze's less than intelligent couriers was taken in a complicated confidence scam by a cripple. He was relieved of $62,000. Now –

(*to all of them*)

It has taken us some time to find you. Our intention was to approach you after your apprehension in New York.

KEATON

You set up the lineup.

KOBAYASHI

Mr Söze made a few calls, yes. You were not to be released until I came to see you. It seems Mr Keaton's attorney, Ms Finneran, was a bit too effective in expediting his release. Holding the rest of you became a moot point.

KEATON

What about Redfoot?

KOBAYASHI

Mr Redfoot knew nothing. Mr Söze rarely works with the same people for very long, and they never know who they're working for. One cannot be betrayed if one has no people.

FENSTER

So why tell us?

KOBAYASHI

Because you have stolen from Mr Söze. That you did not know you stole from him is the only reason you are still alive, but he feels you owe him. You will repay your debt.

HOCKNEY

Who is this guy? How do we know you work for Söze?

KOBAYASHI

I don't think that is relevant, Mr Hockney. The five of you are responsible for the murder of Saul Berg and his bodyguards.

Mr Redfoot can attest to your involvement, and we can see to it that he will. He is not of your 'superior' breed.

MCMANUS

This is a load of shit.

KOBAYASHI

The offer is this, gentlemen. Mr Söze's primary interest, as I am sure you all know, is narcotics. He's been – competing, shall we say, with a group of Argentinians for several years. Competing with Mr Söze has taken its toll. These Argentinians are negotiating the sale of 91 million dollars in cocaine in three days' time. Needless to say, this purchase will revitalize the diminishing strength of their organization. Mr Söze wants you to stop the deal. If you choose, you may wait until the buy. Whatever money changes hands is yours. The transaction will take place on a boat in Marina Del Rey. Mr Söze wants you to take the boat out to sea and sink it with the cocaine on board. When you feel you are safe, you are to inform us of the location of the boat. Then you are free of your obligation to Mr Söze.

KEATON

What if someone else finds the boat?

KOBAYASHI

Then I suggest, Mr Keaton, you sink it where no one will find it, and inform Mr Söze quickly.

Kobayashi puts his briefcase on the table in front of him.

A gift from Mr Söze, gentlemen.

He turns and walks out of the room.

Keaton walks over to the case and opens it. He reaches in and pulls out five thick manilla envelopes, each marked in bold black letters: KEATON, MCMANUS, HOCKNEY, FENSTER and KINT.

Keaton hands each man his file. He opens his first. He pulls out a thick stack of papers and thumbs through them.

KEATON

Jesus Christ. Open them.

All of the men open their files. Inside are mugshots of each man in his respective file as well as a printout of his criminal record. But there is more.

HOCKNEY

They know everything.

MCMANUS

This is my life in here. Everything I've done since I was eighteen.

FENSTER

Everybody I ever worked with, did time with.

HOCKNEY

They fucking know everything.

Keaton pulls out a large black-and-white photograph of himself and his lawyer, Edie Finneran. They are laughing arm-in-arm by a fountain in New York. He hides the photo from the others.

KEATON

This is not right.

FENSTER

I don't know. Who was that guy that used to talk about Söze in New York?

MCMANUS

Bricks Marlin.

FENSTER

Yeah. He said he did jobs for him. Indirect stuff. Always five times more money than the job was worth.

KEATON

Come on. The guy is a pipe dream. This Kobayashi is using him for window dressing.

FENSTER

I don't know. This is bad.

HOCKNEY

It's bullshit. This guy could be LAPD. I think it's a set-up.

FENSTER

The way I hear it, Söze is some kind of butcher. No pity.

KEATON

There is no Keyser Söze.

Verbal thumbs through his file. A long list of names, numbers, addresses. It is a detailed portfolio of his entire criminal and personal life. He looks up at Keaton.

VERBAL

Who is Keyser Söze?

INT. INTERROGATION ROOM – DAY – *PRESENT*

Kujan leans into Verbal's face. He hangs on his every word.

VERBAL

He is supposed to be Turkish. First generation, maybe second. All kinds of stories about him. What he's done, who he's killed. Nobody believed he was real. Nobody ever saw him or knew anybody that ever worked directly for him, but to hear Kobayashi tell it, anybody could have worked for Söze. You never knew. That was his power. The greatest trick the Devil ever pulled was convincing the world he didn't exist. One story the guys told me – the story I believe – was from his days in Turkey. There was this gang of Hungarians that wanted into the mob, any mob. They tried the Chinks and the Guineas. They even tried the Jews – nothing doing. They realized they had no blood and they would never rise to power in another man's mob, so they made their own. After a while they learned the only trick they had. To be in power you didn't need guns or money or numbers. You just needed the will to do what the other guy wouldn't.

INT. TURKISH DELI – DAY

We are in Turkey, perhaps in the early '70s. We see the small Hungarian mob destroying the deli, beating up the proprietor and his wife. One of them cuts off the deli owner's fingers and drops them into the pickle barrel, laughing as he does it.

VERBAL
(*voice-over*)
After a while they come to power, and then they come after Söze. He was small-time then, just running dope, they say.

INT. SÖZE'S HOME – DAY

Three of the Hungarians come bursting into Keyer Söze's home. They grab his five children and round them up in the front room. One of the men grabs Söze's wife and backhands her across the face.

VERBAL
(*voice-over*)
They come to his home in the afternoon looking for his business. They find his wife and kids in the house and decide to wait for Söze.

INT. SÖZE'S HOME – LATER

The front door opens and in walks Keyser Söze. We are never allowed to see his face.

Söze's wife lies in the corner, beaten and bruised. Her dress is tattered to shreds. She cannot look up at her husband.

The three Hungarians stand to greet him. Two hold guns in their hands. The third holds a straight razor. He grabs Söze's youngest boy and holds the razor to his throat.

VERBAL
(*voice-over*)
He comes home to his wife raped and his children screaming. The Hungarians knew Söze was tough. Not to be trifled with. So they let him know they meant business.

The Hungarian smiles. Söze's wife screams in horror.

The Hungarian holds up a blood-soaked razor.

Suddenly, he grabs another child. A little girl no older than six.

They tell Söze they want his territory – all his business. Söze looks over the faces of his family . . . Then he showed these men of will what will really was.

Suddenly, Söze pulls out a pistol and shoots the two men with guns. He turns and aims at the third man holding his child. The man threatens to cut the child's throat, slicing just enough to draw blood.

Söze fires.

The stunned Hungarian watches the child fall from his arms.

Söze turns the pistol on the next child, then the next and the next. He kills his children one by one in front of the Hungarian.

He tells him he would rather see his family dead than live another day after this.

Söze walks over to his wife, crying and beaten on the floor, and holds up her head. She gives him the strangest look. One of trust, perhaps, saturated with fear and humiliation.

He puts the gun between her eyes and fires.

He lets the last Hungarian go, and he goes running. He waits until his wife and kids are in the ground and he goes after the rest of the mob. He kills their kids, he kills their wives, he kills their parents and their parents' friends.

We see glimpses of Keyser Söze's rampage. Bodies upon bodies in homes and in the streets. Then, the fires.

Stores and homes burn, engulfed in flames.

He burns down the houses they live in and the stores they work in, he kills people that owe them money. And like that, he was gone. Underground. No one has ever seen him again. He becomes a myth, a spook story that criminals tell their kids at night. If you rat on your pop, Keyser Söze will get you. And nobody really ever believes.

INT. RABIN'S OFFICE – DAY

KUJAN

Do you believe in him, Verbal?

VERBAL

Keaton always said: 'I don't believe in God, but I'm afraid of him.' Well, I believe in God, and the only thing that scares me is Keyser Söze.

INT. WORKSHOP

Captain Leo listens to Verbal on the speaker with one ear.

LEO

You give this any weight, Agent Briggs?

BRIGGS

I can introduce you to Dan Metzheiser from Justice. He has a file on Söze in DC. It's been a hobby of his for a few years. A lot of guys equate him to that reporter on *The Incredible Hulk*.

LEO

Had *you* heard of him before?

BRIGGS

On the street? A few times. Outside stuff. Somebody was working for a guy who was working for a guy who got money through Keyser Söze. That kind of shit. Could be an old badge. A hex sign to keep people from fucking with you back when a name meant something.

LEO

But you're here.

BRIGGS

Shit, yeah. I got a guy trying to walk out of the hospital on a fried drumstick to get away from Söze. I'll run it up the flagpole.

INT. RABIN'S OFFICE

VERBAL

I came clean. I told it like it happened on the boat. So what if I left out how I got there? It's got so many holes in it, the DA would've told me to blow amnesty out my ass. So you got what you wanted out of me. Big fucking deal.

KUJAN

And this is why you never told the DA.

VERBAL

You tell me, Agent Kujan. If I told you the Loch Ness monster hired me to hit the marina, what would you say?

KUJAN

Turn state's evidence. Take the stand on this and we'll hear it out.

VERBAL

I've got immunity now. What can you possibly offer me?

KUJAN

If there is a Keyser Söze, he'll be looking for you.

VERBAL

Where's your head, Agent Kujan? Where do you think the pressure's coming from? Keyser Söze – or whatever you want to call him – knows where I am right now. He's got the front burner under your ass to let me go so he can scoop me up ten minutes later. Immunity was just to deal with you assholes. I got a whole new problem when I post bail.

KUJAN

He can get you in jail just as easy. Maybe easier.

VERBAL

And outside he can cut me open and find out how much I know. How much I told you.

KUJAN

We can protect you.

VERBAL

Gee, thanks, Dave. Bang-up job so far. Extortion, coercion. You'll pardon me if I ask you to kiss my pucker. The same fuckers that rounded us up and sank us into this mess are telling me they'll bail me out? Fuck you.

(*beat*)

You think you can catch Keyser Söze? You think a guy like that comes this close to getting fingered and sticks his head out? If he comes up for anything, it will be to get rid of me. After that, my guess is you'll never hear from him again.

INT. HOSPITAL ROOM – DAY

Kovash spits out a constant river of Hungarian while Bodi tries to keep up, relaying everything to Tracy Fitzgerald.

She sketches frantically while Daniel Metzheiser looks on.

The composite sketch of Keyser Söze is taking form.

EXT. OCEAN – DAY

A beat-up trawler chugs through the wavy water a few miles off the coast. The shore is a distant streak on the horizon.

A lone fisherman is hauling in a large net as the boat pulls it slowly along. He heaves as hard as he can.

Tiny fish are tangled in the net, shimmering like coins as they struggle to escape. Lower in the net are larger and larger fish, flopping over one another in vain, unable to get free.

The fisherman pulls at the net harder now; something huge is dragging it down. He lashes the net to the stern and leans over the side, grabbing it beneath the water-line and yanking with all his might.

Suddenly, a dead body bobs up in the net, tangled and twisted in the mesh. The fisherman leaps back in shock.

The body is bloated and totally drained of color from days in the water.

It is the man in the checkered bathrobe.

INT. WORKSHOP – DAY

Rabin enters the room with a stack of papers in his hand.

RABIN

So far it's all gold. I can't find a guy named Redfoot, but a Saul Berg did end up in a parking garage downtown last month. No leads on it until now.

LEO

And the hijackings in New York?

RABIN

The guns Hockney snatched we know about. The hijacked plane with the platinum and gold wiring checks out. Nothing on Keaton's truckload of steel.

LEO

Trace the owners. Go as far back as you can.

RABIN

He's got you thinking.

LEO

Mental masturbation is all.

BRIGGS

Hold him for a while.

LEO

Not a chance. Find out who this Redfoot guy is – and I want to know about the lawyer, Kobayashi.

LOUIS

Here we go again.

Leo turns up the speaker. Verbal's voice prattles on.

VERBAL

(*voice-over*)

That was how I ended up in a barbershop quartet in Skokie, Illinois.

INT. RABIN'S OFFICE

KUJAN

This is totally irrelevant.

VERBAL

Ohh, but it's not. If I hadn't been nailed in Illinois for running a three-card monte in between sets, I never would have took off for New York. I never would have met Keaton, see. That barbershop quartet was the reason for everything.

KUJAN

Can we just get back to Kobayashi?

VERBAL

The quartet is part of the bit about Kobayashi. The quartet was in my file, along with every other thing I had done since high school, see? Aliases, middlemen. They saw through it all. They knew me better than I did. They knew all of us.

Kujan looks at his watch.

KUJAN

You're stalling, Verbal.

VERBAL

Give a guy a break, huh?

KUJAN

What happened?

Verbal slumps a bit. He realizes his stalling tactic has failed.

VERBAL

We woke up the next morning and Fenster was gone. He couldn't handle the idea of slumming for Söze. He left a note wishing us good luck and took half the money we'd scraped together.

KUJAN

Then what?

VERBAL

McManus was furious. He was talking about tracking him down and ripping his heart out and all sorts of shit. That night we got the call.

KUJAN

What call?

VERBAL

Kobayashi told us were we could find Fenster.

EXT. BEACH – NIGHT – *TWO WEEKS PRIOR*

Keaton looks out over the ocean and smokes a cigarette.

KEATON

What do you want to do with him?

McManus kneels in the sand. Hockney and Verbal stand behind him, staring at something in front of them.

It is the body of Fred Fenster, literally peppered with bullet holes. McManus stares at him, fighting any flicker of emotion.

MCMANUS

I worked five years with Fenster. More jobs, more money than I can count.

KEATON

I'm sorry, McManus.

MCMANUS

I want to bury him.

KEATON

No time.

McManus springs to his feet and points a pistol at Keaton. Keaton turns to face him and raises his head. McManus might as well be pointing a featherduster.

MCMANUS

YOU WILL FIND TIME. You're not the only one with debts, man.

KEATON

No shovel.

MCMANUS

WITH OUR HANDS.

EXT. BEACH – LATER

They all dig in the sand on the deserted beach with their hands. They are up to their waists in the hole they have scooped out. Fenster's body is a few feet away.

HOCKNEY

This is nuts.

MCMANUS

Dig.

HOCKNEY

This is fucking dry sand, man. When he rots, the surfers'll smell him from a hundred yards out.

MCMANUS

DIG, YOU FUCKER.

Hockney can see that McManus has truly gone over the edge for now. Keaton gives him a look that says don't argue.

HOCKNEY

Keaton, we got to go. They're gonna find him.

KEATON

Dig.

VERBAL

What are we gonna do?

HOCKNEY

I can run. I got no problem with that.

KEATON

They don't seem to have a problem with it, either.

MCMANUS

Nobody runs. I'll kill you if you do.

HOCKNEY

This ain't my boy we're burying. I don't owe anybody.

MCMANUS

We got a deal here.

HOCKNEY

Since when?

MCMANUS

Since tonight. Nobody does one of us without the rest paying back.

HOCKNEY

Fuck that.

KEATON

It's not payback, Hockney.

MCMANUS

It's payback.

KEATON

IT'S NOT PAYBACK. That's not my way and I don't answer to you. It's precaution. You want payback? You want to run? I don't care. I'm going to finish this thing. Not for Fenster, not for anybody else, but for me. This Kobayashi cocksucker isn't going to stand over me.

(*beat*)

All of you can go to hell.

Keaton turns and digs furiously with both hands. Hockney takes a moment and slowly starts to do the same.

The four men dig for Fenster – the first to find some rest.

INT. RABIN'S OFFICE – DAY – *PRESENT*

Verbal smokes with his good hand shaking badly.

KUJAN

And after they killed Fenster, nobody would run?

VERBAL

I wanted to. I thought we could make it.

KUJAN

Why didn't you say anything?

VERBAL

I tried, believe me, but Keaton wouldn't have it. It was too far-fetched for him. Keaton was a grounded guy. An ex-cop. To a cop, the explanation is never that complicated. It's always simple. There's no mystery on the street, no arch-criminal behind it all. If you got a dead guy and you think his brother did it, you're going to find out you're right. Nobody argued with Keaton. They just set their minds on whacking Kobayashi.

EXT. PARKING LOT – NIGHT – *TWO WEEKS PRIOR*

Redfoot's Harley rests on the roof of the Caddy in a mangled heap. The body of the Caddy is riddled with bullet holes.

Redfoot's dead body has been shoved headfirst through a hole in the windshield, recognizable only by the trademark red boot.

INT. OFFICE BUILDING – DAY

Kobayashi walks through the front door of a plush office tower followed by two bodyguards. He heads towards the elevator, failing to notice Hockney a few feet away, reading a newspaper.

We see a wire running from Hockney's ear to his collar.

HOCKNEY

He's coming up.

INT. HALLWAY – 40TH FLOOR

Keaton, McManus and Verbal stand by the six elevators on the 40th floor. They are all wearing khaki overalls and tool belts with walkie-talkies. They look like maintenance men.

All of the elevators have been propped open and stranded.

McManus moves into one of the elevators.

INT. ELEVATOR

McManus reaches over and pulls out the stop button. The elevator doors close. McManus goes to hit the first floor button.

Suddenly, he looks around in surprise. He looks up at the panel that indicates what floor the elevator is on. The numbers are climbing.

MCMANUS

Shit.

(*into radio*)

Keaton, I'm going up.

KEATON

(*on radio*)

Say again.

MCMANUS

I'm going up. Somebody hit the button.

INT. HALLWAY

Keaton looks at Verbal. He grabs his radio.

KEATON

Hockney, where is he?

INT. LOBBY

Hockney glances over his newspaper and sees Kobayashi's bodyguard pushing the elevator button repeatedly.

HOCKNEY

Waiting patiently. Let's get a move on, boys.

INT. ELEVATOR

The elevator stops on the 50th floor. McManus looks around, wondering what to do. The doors open.

A white-haired man in a gray suit gets on. He looks at McManus in the way that most white-haired men in suits look at men in khaki overalls. McManus smiles.

MCMANUS

What floor, sir?

WHITE-HAIRED MAN

Lobby, please.

McManus fights to maintain a friendly smile. This is obviously the worst floor he could have chosen.

McManus looks at the buttons. Two rows of thirty buttons numbered 1 to 60. McManus presses the one marked L.

INT. HALLWAY

Keaton and Verbal listen for anything on the radio.

INT. LOBBY

One of Kobayashi's bodyguards summons a security guard.

INT. ELEVATOR

McManus watches the numbers on the panel. They are fifteen floors away from the lobby now. McManus is fidgeting. The white-haired man looks at him out of the corner of his eye with great distaste.

McManus suddenly smiles. He reaches out with his index and middle fingers and runs them down the two rows of buttons. With the flick of his hand, he has hit every floor between them and the lobby.

He looks at the white-haired man and smiles wider.

The elevator stops on the 10th floor and the white-haired man gets off with a sneer for McManus.

The doors close behind him. McManus scrambles for the ceiling hatch.

INT. LOBBY

Hockney is watching Kobayashi's bodyguards argue with the security guard.

HOCKNEY
(*into radio*)
It's getting busy down here.

Suddenly, the elevator opens. Hockney lets out a sigh of relief. Kobayashi and his bodyguards get on the elevator.

INT. ELEVATOR

The elevator is empty except for the three men. McManus has vanished. Kobayashi presses a button and they are on their way.

Suddenly, the ceiling hatch opens and McManus's arm comes out.

POP – POP: *Two shots from a suppressed pistol and the guards drop to the floor, dead.*

Kobayashi looks up with surprising calm into McManus's barrel.

MCMANUS

Press 40.

INT. HALLWAY – 40TH FLOOR

The elevator opens and Kobayashi is greeted by Keaton and Verbal. McManus drops from the ceiling hatch and pushes him out.

Verbal and McManus grab the dead bodies and pull them out of the elevator. They drag them to the next elevator, which has been forced open, revealing an empty shaft.

Verbal and McManus throw the bodies down the shaft. Kobayashi watches this without any evident emotion as the door closes.

KEATON

The answer is no.

KOBAYASHI

Mr Söze will be most –

KEATON

Listen to me, cocksucker. There is no Keyser Söze. If you say his name again, I'll kill you right here.

KOBAYASHI

A strange threat. I can only assume you're here to kill me anyway. Pity about Mr Redfoot.

MCMANUS

Fair trade for Fenster.

The elevator opens and Hockney steps out.

KOBAYASHI

Ahh, Mr Hockney. Do join us.

KEATON

We know you can get to us, and now you know we can get to you. I'm offering you the chance to call this off.

KOBAYASHI

Mr Sö – my employer has made up his mind. He does not change it.

KEATON

Neither do we.

MCMANUS

You got Fenster, you may get more, but you won't get us all. Not before one of us gets to you.

KOBAYASHI

I believe you, Mr McManus. I quite sincerely do. You would not have been chosen if you were not so capable, but I cannot make this decision. Whatever you can threaten me with is . . . ludicrous in comparison to what will be done to me if I do not carry out my orders in full.

MCMANUS

Just so you know. I'm the guy. I'm the one that's gonna get through to you.

KOBAYASHI

I *am* sorry, Mr McManus.

(*to Keaton*)

I implore you to believe me, Mr Keaton. Mr Söze is very real and very determined.

KEATON

We'll see.

McManus holds a pistol to Kobayashi's chin. The lawyer's cool eyes never falter.

KOBAYASHI

Before you do me in, you will let me finish my business with Ms Finneran first, won't you?

Suddenly, Keaton grabs McManus's hand and pulls the gun away before he can shoot.

KEATON

What did you say?

KOBAYASHI

Edie Finneran. She is upstairs in my office for an extradition deposition. I requested she be put on the case personally. She flew out yesterday.

Everyone looks at Keaton.

No matter. Kill away, Mr McManus.

KEATON

You're lying.

KOBAYASHI

Am I?

INT. HALLWAY – 50TH FLOOR

Everyone follows Kobayashi quietly down a dimly lit, oak-lined hallway. Verbal holds a small pistol discreetly in the small of Kobayashi's back.

They come to a glass-enclosed office foyer. Kobayashi gestures and everyone looks through the glass into the lobby beyond.

Edie Finneran is talking casually with the receptionist.

INT. LOBBY

Edie glances toward the men in the hall.

Keaton turns quickly on his heels, facing the others. From where Edie stands, it looks as though Kobayashi is talking to a group of harmless maintenance men.

They see a large man dressed very much like the two dead bodies left down the elevator shaft. The man notices Kobayashi and the others. He stands and stares menacingly.

KOBAYASHI

Ms Finneran's escort in Los Angeles. Never leaves her for a moment. I thought you'd like to know she was in good hands.

Keaton's mind races for an alternative. He can find none. Verbal lowers his gun without being told.

Get your rest, gentlemen. The boat will be ready for you on Friday. If I see you or your friends before then, or fail to check in every half hour with that unpleasant looking man in there, Ms Finneran will find herself the victim of a gruesome violation before she dies. As will your father, Mr Hockney –

and your Uncle Randall in Arizona, Mr Kint. I might only castrate Mr McManus's nephew, David. Do I make myself clear?

All of the men surround Kobayashi, aching to kill him.

I'll take care of the dead men downstairs. We'll add them to the cost of Mr Fenster. Now, if you'll excuse me.

Kobayashi walks into the office. Edie turns to greet him. Keaton slowly turns and watches as they shake hands and talk. Kobayashi says something they cannot hear and Edie laughs, her back to the window.

Kobayashi smiles over her shoulder at Keaton.

All the while, the bodyguard watches Keaton. He nods politely before Keaton and the others leave. Verbal watches for a moment more and follows.

INT. HOTEL ROOM – NIGHT

Another file from Kobayashi's briefcase is laid out on the table. This has a map and a good fifty pages of information in it.

KEATON

It's a logistical nightmare. Close quarters, no advance layout, ten men, maybe twenty.

HOCKNEY

Can we stealth these guys?

KEATON

Doubtful. With all that coke, they'll be ready – which brings me to sunny spot number two. Even if *one* of us gets through and jacks the boat, we get nothing.

MCMANUS

And if we wait for the money?

KEATON

Ten more men at least. In my opinion, it can't be done. Anyone who walks into this won't come out alive.

MCMANUS

I'm for waiting for the money.

HOCKNEY

Me, too.

VERBAL

Did you hear what he just said?

HOCKNEY

If I'm going in, I want a stake.

VERBAL

But we can't do it.

MCMANUS

We *have* to do it. What's with you, man?

VERBAL

I just can't believe we're gonna walk into certain death.

Pause. They all suddenly realize the weight of their situation.

Finally:

MCMANUS

News said it's raining in New York.

No one knows quite how to respond.

EXT. PIER – MARINA DEL REY – NIGHT

A large boat, sleek and yachtlike, but without finesse. This is a boat for business – heavy and fast. It is moored to the pier.

A large crane hoists a pallet of fuel drums from the dock. It swings slowly over the boat. A man on the dock yells in Spanish to the crane operator.

A black van pulls up to the boat. A group of men in suits walk down the pier and along the side of the boat. They call out in a strange language to the man on dock.

EXT. WAREHOUSE

Behind an old and weathered building, Keaton and Verbal watch the boat from the shadows.

VERBAL

What are they speaking?

KEATON

Russian. I think. I don't know.

VERBAL

Hungarian?

KEATON

Knock it off.

EXT. PIER

Five men come up from below deck. They are tense and cautious around the men in suits. Someone speaks in Spanish and someone else in Russian. It takes a moment before anyone speaks the same tongue. They settle on French for both negotiators.

EXT. MARINA

Another van is parked a hundred yards away in the shadows.

INT. VAN

Hockney sits in the van. He picks up a walkie-talkie.

HOCKNEY

Are we ready, kids?

INT. WAREHOUSE

McManus is crawling through the top rafters of the warehouse. He makes his way to a window in the top where the two halves of the roof join. He lugs a heavy rifle. He stops and grabs his radio.

MCMANUS

If I didn't have to stop and answer you, I would be.

EXT. WAREHOUSE

KEATON

Everyone shut up. I'm ready. McManus, you better be set up in ten seconds.

MCMANUS
(*on radio*)

Don't wait for me.

KEATON

Make sure someone has my back.

VERBAL

I'm there.

Verbal holds up a subgun. Keaton smiles bitterly. He moves to step into the open and stops.

KEATON

I want you to stay here. Understand?

VERBAL

But I thought I –

KEATON

Cover us from here. If we don't make it out, I want you to take the money and go.

VERBAL
(*confused*)

Keaton, I can't just –

KEATON

I want you to find Edie. Both of you find some place safe. Tell her what happened – everything. She knows people. She'll know what to do. If we can't get Kobayashi my way, she'll get him her way.

VERBAL

What if I –

KEATON

Just do what I tell you.

Keaton turns and takes a few steps. He stops and looks back, his face marked with guilt and agony.

Tell her I . . . Tell her I tried.

Keaton leaves before Verbal can respond. He walks out toward the boat.

He is no more than three feet out of the shadows before the first man sees him.

EXT. PIER

One of the men in suits starts to yell to the others. Men pull out guns and try to look as cool as they can.

Keaton walks right into the face of all of these men, undaunted. His hands are in his pockets.

Above him, in the darkness, a small window opens at the top of the warehouse. McManus pokes his head out and spies Keaton. He pulls his head in and sticks out the barrel of the rifle.

Keaton marches toward them. The men on the boat jump up onto the pier to join the men in suits. Keaton comes to a stop about twenty feet from fifteen men standing together.

INT. WAREHOUSE

McManus's POV*: McManus stares through the scope of his rifle at the scene. The crosshair breezes past Keaton and finds a target. A man in a suit.*

MCMANUS

Pow.

He moves to another and then another, picking up speed and mock-shooting the men. He is steady and quick. It is clear he could take all fifteen in a few seconds.

Pow-pow-pow-pow-pow-pow. Oswald was a fag.

EXT. PIER

The men shout questions at Keaton in a number of languages.

INT. VAN

Hockney bails out and runs quickly and quietly through the shadows.

EXT. WAREHOUSE

Verbal aims his subgun and clicks off the safety.

INT. WAREHOUSE

McManus still wanders with his scope.

MCMANUS

Old McDonald had a farm, ee-aye, ee-aye, ohh. And on this farm he shot some guys. Ba-da-bing, ba-da-bip, bang-boom.

EXT. PIER

Finally, two men walk right toward Keaton. The rest train guns on him. They reach for his arms, pointing their guns right at him.

BOOM-BOOM: Two shots, rapid fire, take their heads off.

INT. WAREHOUSE

MCMANUS

ELVIS HAS LEFT THE BUILDING.

He fires as fast as he can.

EXT. PIER

Keaton pulls a pistol out of each pocket and aims at whatever moves. He fires and runs for cover.

The men from the boat and the men in suits try to peg him, but McManus's sniping has them running.

Suddenly, Hockney joins Keaton. They fire in all directions. Verbal shoots from his position in the shadows. He is all over the place, hardly able to control the gun. Still, he makes an impressive and violent display, filling the air with bullets.

The pier is a mass of running, shooting, dead or dying men. It is total pandemonium. A killing spree let loose by those with the will to do what the other guys would not.

INT. CRANE

The crane operator opens the door to bail out. He looks down at the gunfight and thinks better of it. He tries his best to slip down between the seat and the panel.

EXT. WAREHOUSE

McManus comes repelling down the front of the warehouse. He is facing forward, one hand behind his back to feed the rope out behind him, the other hand firing a subgun.

EXT. PIER

Hockney is running straight for the boat when he suddenly stops. He glances over his shoulder at the van brought by the men in suits.

He looks ahead at McManus and Keaton blazing for the boat.

Finally, he turns and runs back for the van. He shoots a man point blank in the face and runs over his body as it falls.

He gets to the back door of the van and yanks it open. The inside is stacked with large wooden crates.

INT. VAN

Hockney laughs and jumps in, suddenly oblivious to the sound of gunfire. He opens one of the crates and looks inside.

It is filled with money. Cash and negotiable bonds of all kinds.

He smiles.

BOOM: *Blood sprays all over the money. Hockney looks at it, puzzled.*

He turns and sees one of the men in suits holding a shotgun.

Hockney looks down at his own open belly, blood and innards flowing freely.

BOOM: *Another shot takes off the top of his head.*

EXT. PIER

McManus runs like a wild man across the dock, heading for the boat.

He shoots in all directions as though he has eyes in the back of his head. He sees Keaton climbing onto the deck of the boat.

MCMANUS

KEATON. ON YOUR SIX.

Keaton hears this and spins on his heels in time to see one of the boat men behind him. He fires and kills him instantly.

EXT. WAREHOUSE

Verbal is wrestling with a new magazine for his gun. He has a great deal of difficulty getting it in. He fumbles with the gun and it goes off, spitting rounds everywhere.

EXT. CRANE

A single bullet hits one of the barrels on the suspended pallet. Gasoline pours out through the bullet hole.

INT. CRANE

Stray bullets pepper the glass on the cabin of the crane. The operator is hit. He slumps forward, dead, hitting the lever and bringing the crane around.

It wheels slowly toward the boat, swinging the pallet of fuel drums with it.

EXT. BOAT

Keaton finds the hatch and goes below, shooting a man on his way up the stairs. McManus jumps on board and runs down behind him.

EXT. WAREHOUSE

Verbal watches them vanish. He hears the muffled sound of gunfire below deck. He walks out from behind the warehouse and limps slowly across the pier.

It is quiet, except for the sounds of screaming, far off in the bowels of the boat, and the hum of the crane.

Suddenly, Verbal turns – just in time to see the crane swinging around. The pallet is headed right at him.

He ducks at the last possible second and it swoops past, continuing on in a circle.

Verbal breathes quietly. He looks over at the van with the money inside. He looks back at the boat. He stands on the dock, surrounded by the dead, wondering what to do next.

INT. RABIN'S OFFICE – DAY *PRESENT*

KUJAN

Why didn't you run?

VERBAL

I froze up. I thought about Fenster and how he looked when we buried him, then I thought about Keaton. It looked like he might pull it off.

A knock at the door.

Rabin steps in and motions for Kujan to come outside.

INT. HALLWAY

Jasper Briggs and Leo are in the hall. Leo hands Kujan a thick manilla folder. Kujan thumbs through it.

RABIN

A fisherman pulled a stiff out of the water this morning. Thrown clear when the boat exploded. Shot once in the head. Two guys from the DEA identified him an hour ago.

KUJAN

And?

RABIN

His name was Arturo Marquez. A petty smuggler out of Argentina. He was arrested in New York last year for trafficking. He escaped to California and got picked up in Long Beach. They were setting up his extradition when he escaped again. Get this – Edie Finneran was called in to advise the proceedings.

KUJAN

Kobayashi.

RABIN

So it seems.

BRIGGS

I called Manhattan County and they faxed me a copy of the guy's testimony. He was a rat.

Kujan pulls out page after page from the file.

KUJAN

A big fucking rat.

RABIN

Arturo was strongly opposed to going back to prison. So much so that he informed on close to fifty guys. Guess who he names for a finale?

Kujan finds one sheet and notices a paragraph is highlighted.

KUJAN

Keyser Söze.

RABIN

There's more.

INT. RABIN'S OFFICE – MOMENTS LATER

Kujan walks in and sits down in front of Verbal. He smiles.

KUJAN

I'll tell you what I know. Stop me when it sounds familiar.

Verbal is confused.

There was no dope on that boat.

INT. BOAT – NIGHT – *ONE WEEK PRIOR*

Keaton is weaving through tight, low-ceiling corridors, looking in every cabin, working his way toward the bottom of the boat.

Elsewhere in the boat, McManus is tearing through the corridors, seemingly less interested in securing the cargo than he is in killing everyone on board.

He screams like a lunatic, shooting everything in his path, killing some men with his bare hands, shooting others, stabbing still others with a knife he has brought along.

INT. CORRIDOR

Jaime, one of the men from the boat, is half-pushing, half-helping a thin and sweaty-looking man in a checkered bathrobe toward a cabin at the end of the hall.

The man in the robe is trembling. He seems stricken with fear.

MAN IN ROBE

He's here. I saw him on deck.

Jaime pushes him inside the cabin and shuts the door. The man in the robe screams through the closed door, his voice echoing off of the metal bulkheads.

I'M TELLING YOU IT'S KEYSER SÖZE.

Jaime stands outside the door of the cabin and turns to face down the hall. Off in some other part of the boat, he can hear McManus wailing like a banshee and the ever-less-frequent sound of gunfire.

INT. HOLD.

Keaton has come to the four-foot-high door to the hold. The door is open slightly. Keaton finds this strange. He pushes the door open and steps inside. The hold is empty.

He hears a noise behind him. He wheels around to fire. He sees McManus in the door. His face is covered with blood.

MCMANUS

Did you hear what I heard?

KEATON

What happened to you?

MCMANUS

Keyser Söze is on the boat.

KEATON

What?

MCMANUS

I heard somebody screaming his nuts off. He said Keyser Söze was on the boat.

KEATON

Are you all right?

McManus rubs some of the blood off with his sleeve.

MCMANUS

Huh? Oh, it's not mine.

KEATON

There's no coke.

McManus looks around the hold as though he'll see four-and-a-half tons of dope in some corner where Keaton might have missed it.

The two men look at one another. There is a long, pregnant silence.

MCMANUS

Let's get the fuck out of here.

KEATON

Right behind you.

INT. CORRIDOR

Keaton and McManus step out of the hold, walking slowly and cautiously back from where they came. They hear the sounds of running feet on the deck above and the occasional hollered sentence in Spanish.

KEATON

Where's Hockney?

MCMANUS

I don't think he made it to the boat.

They come to a corner. They can go left or right.

KEATON

I can't remember which way.

MCMANUS

Right –

BOOM – BOOM: Gunshots fill the hallway from behind them. They do not stop to turn around. Keaton goes left. McManus goes right. They run in opposite directions with the sound of gunfire right behind them.

INT. HALLWAY – CABIN

Jaime squints and cocks his head.

Someone is coming. He raises a pistol and crouches by the door.

INT. CABIN

The man in the robe sits on the foot of the bed watching the door. He hears the sounds of fighting somewhere not too far away.

He crawls over the bed and squeezes between it and the bulkhead. Only the top of his head is visible. He starts to cry.

BOOM – BOOM: Two shots just outside in the hall.

Suddenly, the door bursts open. Jaime collapses in a heap on the floor, a bullet hole in his eye.

A figure looms in the door.

The man in the robe looks up at the man. We cannot see him.

MAN IN ROBE

I told them nothing.

BOOM: The man in the robe falls dead.

EXT. DECK – MOMENTS LATER

The boat is quiet now. Keaton walks out onto the deck and starts to free the lines that secure the boat to the dock.

He looks out over the pier and sees Verbal standing in the middle of the carnage, frozen. Their eyes meet. Keaton waves at him as if to shoo him away.

EXT. PIER

Verbal hesitates and finally moves toward the van with the money. He looks back over his shoulder and sees Keaton freeing the last line of the boat. Keaton sees him looking and waves again, hurrying him along.

Verbal turns away and focuses on the van.

EXT. DECK

Keaton hears a noise behind him. He swings around and points his gun at McManus again. He puts the gun down.

McManus smiles. He walks slowly across the deck toward Keaton. Something is not right about him.

MCMANUS

Strangest thing.

He slumps to the deck. Keaton rushes over to him. He kneels down and sees a pipe sticking out of the back of McManus's neck.

EXT. PIER

As Verbal approaches the van, he looks to his left at the huge loading crane. He glances upward along the giant arm as it swings steadily on.

Somewhere, off in the distance, the sound of sirens can be heard.

EXT. DECK

Keaton kneels by McManus, trembling with rage. After a moment he stands, looking down at McManus's dead body.

EXT. PIER

Suddenly, Verbal realizes something. He turns and goes to call out a warning to Keaton. He is too late.

EXT. DECK

Keaton never sees the crane coming.

WHAM: *The pallet of barrels hits him square in the back and sends him flying into the wheelhouse of the boat.*

EXT. PIER

Verbal runs toward the boat as fast as he can.

Suddenly, he stops dead in his tracks.

From where he stands, he can just make out the figure of a tall, thin man on the pier. The man moves quietly and calmly in the shadows toward the crane, looking out of place in his expensive suit.

Verbal strains, but he cannot see this man's face. Yet we know he knows who he is.

Something about this man terrifies him beyond belief.

EXT. DECK

Keaton is still for a moment. Finally, he tries to move, but finds he cannot move his legs. A large cut runs the length of his face, bleeding badly. He manages to move himself with great effort into a sitting position, leaning against the wheelhouse.

This is where we found him in the beginning.

Keaton looks down toward the end of the boat and sees the pallet swing around to a stop.

Suddenly, it lowers to the deck on the stern.

Someone has gotten control of the crane.

The first trickling of the stream of gasoline from the leaking barrel flows past Keaton's strangely angled feet. He slumps back and looks up at the dark night sky.

Sirens in the distance grow slightly louder.

INT. RABIN'S OFFICE – DAY – *PRESENT*

KUJAN

And that's when you say in your statement that you saw . . .

Kujan picks up his copy of Verbal's statement to the DA.

A man in a suit with a slim build. Tall.

VERBAL

Wait a minute.

KUJAN

(*looking at watch*)

I don't have a minute. Are you saying it was Keyser Söze? You told the DA you didn't know who it was.

Verbal is drowning in Kujan's interrogation. He looks dazed.

VERBAL

I – there had to be dope there.

KUJAN

Don't shine me, Verbal. No more stalling. You know what I'm getting at.

VERBAL

I don't.

KUJAN

YES YOU DO. YOU KNOW WHAT I'M GETTING AT. THE TRUTH. TRY TO TELL ME YOU DIDN'T KNOW. TRY TO TELL ME YOU SAW SOMEONE KILL KEATON.

For the first time, Verbal stands and tries to move away from Kujan, but Kujan stays in his face, backing him into a corner. Verbal shields himself with his hands and shuts his eyes.

TRY TO KEEP LYING TO ME NOW. I KNOW EVERYTHING.

VERBAL

I don't know what you're talking about.

KUJAN

YOU KNOW. YOU'VE KNOWN THIS WHOLE FUCKING TIME. GIVE IT TO ME.

Verbal looks into Kujan's eyes with genuine terror. Kujan's face is red, his body trembles. His locomotive breathing is the only sound in the room.

VERBAL

I don't understand what you're saying. I saw Keaton get shot, I swear to you.

KUJAN

Then *why* didn't you help him?

VERBAL

I WAS AFRAID, OKAY? Somehow, I was sure it was Keyser Söze at that point. I couldn't bring myself to raise my gun to him.

KUJAN

But Keaton . . .

VERBAL

It was Keyser Söze, Agent Kujan. I mean the Devil himself. How do you shoot the Devil in the back?

Verbal holds up a shaking, twisted hand.

What if you miss?

EXT. PIER – NIGHT – *ONE WEEK PRIOR*

Verbal is in the shadows, watching as the man in a suit strides across the deck over to Keaton, stopping to relieve himself on a small fire on the deck.

He walks up and stands over Keaton. The two men exchange words and the man in the suit pulls out a pistol. He points it at Keaton's head.

Red and blue lights flash behind Verbal.

Verbal turns. He can just make out two police cars coming in the distance. He runs for cover, hiding in the tangle of tubes and metal struts at the base of the crane.

BANG: *Verbal hears a shot from the deck of the boat. He turns in time to see the man in the suit running across the deck toward the gangway.*

Verbal can barely see the man from where he is now. Keaton's body is completely obscured at this angle. The man in the suit is covered by shadows and the poor angle from behind the crane. Verbal strains to see but he cannot.

The man in the suit stops long enough to pull out a lighter. He bends down to the deck of the boat and ignites the gasoline. He runs off as more police cars arrive.

Lights flood the pier.

Police are everywhere. The sound of radios and running feet fill the air.

A bright light shines directly on Verbal from behind.

VOICE
(*off-screen*)
DON'T MOVE. LET ME SEE YOUR HANDS.

Verbal does as he is told.

INT. RABIN'S OFFICE – DAY – *PRESENT*

KUJAN
Arturo Marquez. Ever hear of him?

VERBAL
Wha – No.

KUJAN
He was a stool pigeon for the Justice Department. He swore out a statement to Federal Marshals that he had seen and could positively identify one Keyser Söze and had intimate knowledge of his business, including, but not exclusive to, drug trafficking and murder.

VERBAL
I never heard of him.

KUJAN
His own people were selling him – to a gang of Hungarians. Most likely the same Hungarians that Söze all but wiped out back in Turkey. The money wasn't there for dope. The Hungarians were going to *buy* the one guy that could finger Söze for them.

VERBAL
I said I never heard of him.

KUJAN
But Keaton had. Edie Finneran was his extradition advisor. She knew who he was and what he knew.

VERBAL

I don't –

KUJAN

There were no drugs on that boat. It was a hit. A suicide mission to whack out the one man that could finger Keyser Söze, so Söze had a few thieves put to it. Men he knew he could march into certain death.

VERBAL

But how – wait. You're saying Söze sent us to kill someone?

KUJAN

I'm saying Keaton did.

Verbal cannot grasp this. He squints, trying to understand.

Verbal, he left you behind for a reason. If you all knew Söze could find you anywhere, why was he ready to send you off with the money when he could have used you to take the boat?

VERBAL

He wanted me to live.

KUJAN

Why did he want you to live? A one-time dirty cop without a loyalty in the world finds it in his heart to save a worthless rat-cripple? No, sir. Why?

VERBAL

Edie.

KUJAN

I don't buy that reform story for a minute. And even if I did, I certainly don't believe he would send *you* to protect her. So why?

VERBAL

Because he was my friend.

KUJAN

No, Verbal. You weren't friends. Keaton didn't have friends. He saved you because he wanted it that way. It was his will.

Verbal grinds to a mental halt, trying to grasp the implication.

Suddenly:

VERBAL

No . . .

KUJAN

Keaton was Keyser Söze.

VERBAL

NO.

KUJAN

The kind of guy who could wrangle the wills of men like Hockney and McManus. The kind of man who could engineer a police lineup from all his years of contacts in the NYPD.

Verbal stands on wobbly legs, shaking with anger.

VERBAL

NO, NO, NO, NO, NO.

KUJAN

THE KIND OF MAN THAT COULD HAVE KILLED EDIE FINNERAN.

A strange look crosses Verbal's face. Shock, perhaps, or revelation.

They found her yesterday in a hotel in Pennsylvania. Shot twice in the head.

It starts to sink in with Verbal. His eyes swell.

VERBAL

Edie . . .

KUJAN

He used all of you to get him on that boat. He couldn't get on alone and he had to pull the trigger himself to make sure he got his man. The *one* man that could identify him.

VERBAL

This is all bullshit.

KUJAN

He left you to stay behind and tell us he was dead. You saw him die, right? Or did you? You had to hide when the first police cars showed up. You heard the shot just before the fire but you *didn't see him die.*

VERBAL

I knew him. He would never –

KUJAN

He programmed you to tell us just what he wanted you to. Customs has been investigating him for years. He knew we were close. You said it yourself. Where is the political pressure coming from? Why are you being protected? It's Keaton making sure you tell us what you're supposed to. Immunity is your reward.

VERBAL

BUT WHY ME? WHY NOT HOCKNEY OR FENSTER OR MCMANUS? I'm a cripple. I'm stupid. Why me?

Verbal hears the weight of his words and falls back in his chair. Kujan looks at him with some pity, but he is too far in to stop.

KUJAN

Because you're a cripple, Verbal. *Because* you're stupid. Because you were weaker than them. Because you couldn't see far enough into him to know the truth.

Verbal is crying now. He shakes his head, eyes closed.

If he's dead, Verbal – if what you say is true, then it won't matter. It *was* his idea to hit the Taxi Service in New York, wasn't it? Tell me the truth.

VERBAL

(*sobbing*)

It was all Keaton. We followed him from the beginning.

Kujan smiles with triumphant satisfaction.

I didn't know. I saw him die. I believe he's dead. Christ –

KUJAN

Why lie about everything else then?

VERBAL

You know what it's like, Agent Kujan, to know you'll never be good? Not good like you. You got good all fucked around. I mean a stand-up guy. I grew up knowing I was never going to be good at anything 'cause I was a cripple. Shit, I wasn't even a good thief. But I thought the one thing I could be good at was keeping my mouth shut – keeping the code. I didn't want to tell you for my dignity, that's all, and you robbed me, Agent Kujan. You robbed me.

Kujan puts the coffee mug on the desk and holds up the microphone. Verbal actually manages to snort a laugh, but only briefly, overcome by an apparent wave of nausea.

KUJAN

You're not safe on your own.

VERBAL

You think he's . . .

KUJAN

Is he Keyser Söze? I don't know, Verbal. It seems to me that Keyser Söze is a shield. Like you said, a spook story, but I know Keaton – and someone out there is pulling strings for you. Stay here and let us protect you.

VERBAL

I'm not bait. No way. I post today.

KUJAN

You posted twenty minutes ago. Captain Leo wants you out of here ASAP, unless you turn state's.

VERBAL

I'll take my chances, thank you. It's tougher to buy the cheapest bag-man than it is to buy a cop.

KUJAN

Where are you going to go, Verbal? You gonna run? Turn state's evidence. You might never see trial. If somebody wants to get you, you *know* they'll get you out there.

VERBAL

Maybe so, but I'm no rat, Agent Kujan. You tricked me, is all. I won't keep my mouth shut 'cause I'm scared. I'll keep it shut 'cause that's the way. I let Keaton down by getting caught – Edie Finneran, too. And if they kill me, it's because they'll hear I dropped dime. They'll probably hear it from you.

Verbal stands, mustering his shattered dignity and walks toward the door. Rabin opens it for him from outside.

For once, Kujan cannot bring himself to look at Verbal.

Verbal turns to the door, stopping to look Rabin in the eye.

Fuckin' cops.

He steps out of the room and into the hall. Rabin follows him.

INT. HOSPITAL – DAY

Daniel Metzheiser comes out of Arkosh Kovash's room with a single sheet of fifteen by twenty-inch paper in his hand. He inspects the sketch with great interest. He folds the edges of the paper back to make it smaller.

INT. HOSPITAL RECEPTION ROOM

Metzheiser walks behind the reception desk without asking the nurse for permission and helps himself to the fax machine.

INT. DEPOT – LATER

Verbal is downstairs in the depot of the police station, picking up his personal belongings.

A fat, white-haired cop is checking off the items as he takes them out of the tray in which they are kept.

COP

One watch: gold. One cigarette lighter: gold. One wallet: brown –

From far down the hall, Captain Leo watches as Verbal collects his personal items and shuffles on his lame leg toward the exit.

INT. DISPATCHER'S OFFICE

Jasper Briggs stands by a fax machine. A green light comes on next to a digital display.

The display reads: RECEIVING

INT. RABIN'S OFFICE

Kujan stares solemnly at the bulletin board, drinking from Rabin's coffee cup. Rabin sits at the desk, sifting through the mound of papers as though considering organizing them once and for all.

RABIN

You still don't know shit.

KUJAN

I know what I wanted to know about Keaton.

RABIN

Which is shit.

KUJAN

No matter. He'll have to know how close we came.

RABIN

Keyser Söze or not, if Keaton's alive he'll never come up again.

KUJAN

I'll find him.

RABIN

Waste of time.

KUJAN

(*to himself*)

A rumor is not a rumor that doesn't die.

RABIN

What?

KUJAN

Nothing. Something I – forget it.

Kujan shakes his head. He gestures to the desk.

Man, you're a fucking slob.

Rabin regards the mess of his office.

RABIN

Yeah. It's got its own system, though. It all makes sense when you look at it right. You just have to step back from it, you know? You should see my garage, now that's a horror show . . .

Kujan is not listening. He has been staring at the bulletin board, lost in thought, his unfocused eyes drifting across the mess of papers, not looking at anything at all.

EXT. STREET

Verbal steps out into the sunlight, putting on a pair of cheap sunglasses. He looks up and down the crowded street. People on their way to and from lunch, no doubt.

Cars choke the street in front of the police station, waiting for pedestrians to clear the way.

INT. DISPATCHER'S OFFICE

A single sheet of paper comes out of the fax machine, facedown.

INT. RABIN'S OFFICE

Kujan still stares at the bulletin board.

Suddenly, Kujan's face changes. He leans in closer to the bulletin board and squints his eyes. His face changes again.

First a look of puzzlement, then confusion – finally realization.

The coffee cup tumbles from his hand. It hits the floor with the smash of cheap porcelain. Coffee splatters everywhere.

Rabin snaps out of his droning and looks up in surprise.

Kujan's POV: *Kujan staring not at what is on the bulletin board, but at the bulletin board itself.*

His eyes follow the aluminum frame, mounted firmly to the wall. One might note its sturdy construction and its convenient size. Big enough to hold a lifetime of forgotten and disregarded notes and facts. Years of police trivia that has been hung and forgotten with the intention of finding a use for it all someday. One might want such a bulletin board for oneself. One would look to see who makes such a bulletin board.

Kujan's eyes are locked on a metal plate bearing the manufacturer's name.

It reads: QUARTET – SKOKIE, ILLINOIS.

Kujan's eyes flash all over the bulletin board. He finds a picture of Rabin in the far corner. He stands beside a scale in fishing gear. He proudly holds a hand out to his freshly caught Marlin. His eyes skin quickly over and stop on an eight and a half by eleven-inch fax sheet of what must be a 300lb black man. Kujan glazes over his name; it is irrelevant. His aliases stand out.

Slavin, BRICKS, *Shank,* REDFOOT, *Theo, Rooster . . .*

Kujan's eyes widen with sudden realization. He runs for the door. His foot crushes the broken pieces of Rabin's coffee cup. The cup that hovered over Verbal's head for two hours.

Kujan is in too much of a hurry to notice the two words printed on the jagged piece that had been the bottom of the cheap mug: KOBAYASHI PORCELAIN.

INT. HALLWAY

Kujan is sprinting wildly down the hall for the stairs.

EXT. STREET

Verbal looks behind him and sees Captain Leo standing just inside the doorway, watching him in the way that cops look at people they cannot place in the category of idiot citizen or stupid criminal. Verbal smiles politely, meekly at Leo and walks down the steps into the moving throng.

INT. DEPOT

Kujan runs past the fat, white-haired cop at the desk where Verbal had only moments before picked up his belongings. Rabin is right behind him, a look of absolute confusion on his face.

EXT. POLICE STATION

Captain Leo stands in the doorway, enjoying a cigarette. Kujan nearly barrels into him.

KUJAN

WHERE IS HE? DID YOU SEE HIM?

LEO

The cripple? He went that way.

Leo gestures toward the vast crowd on its way everywhere.

Kujan runs into the crowd, looking around frantically.

EXT. SIDEWALK

Verbal limps his way carefully across the sidewalk, avoiding people as best as he can.

He looks over his shoulder, getting farther away from the police station. He can see Captain Leo and Rabin on the steps, looking around with strange, lost expressions on their faces.

He does not notice the car creeping along the curb beside him.

INT. CAR

Driver's POV: *The driver's hands tap the wheel patiently. His eyes follow Verbal as he fumbles through the crowd.*

EXT. SIDEWALK

Kujan pushes and shoves, looking this way and that.

EXT. STREET

Low angle on the feet of hundreds of people.

Verbal's feet emerge from the crowd on the far side. They hobble along the curb.

Suddenly, the right foot seems to relax a little, the inward angle straightens itself out in a few paces and the limp ceases as though the leg has grown another inch.

Crane up Verbal's body.

Verbal's hands are rummaging around in his pockets. The good left hand comes up with a pack of cigarettes, the bad right hand comes up with a lighter. The right hand flexes with all of the grace and coordination of a sculptor's, flicking the clasp on the antique lighter with the thumb, striking the flint with the index finger. It is a fluid motion, somewhat showy.

Verbal lights a cigarette and smiles to himself. He turns and sees the car running alongside.

INT. DISPATCHER'S OFFICE

Jasper Briggs pulls the sheet out of the fax machine and turns it over, revealing the composite sketch of Keyser Söze.

Though crude and distorted, one cannot help but notice how much it looks like Verbal Kint.

EXT. STREET

The car stops. The driver gets out.

It is Kobayashi, or the man we have come to know as such. He smiles to Verbal. Verbal steps off the curb, returning the smile as he opens the passenger door and gets in.

The man called Kobayashi gets in the driver's seat and pulls away.

A moment later, Agent David Kujan of US Customs wanders into the frame, looking around much in the way a child would when lost at the circus. He takes no notice of the car pulling out into traffic, blending in with the rest of the cars filled with people on their way back to work.

BLACK.